ROBINSON CRUSOE, USN

AMERICA READS

Rediscovered Fiction and Nonfiction from Key Periods in American History

THE GREAT DEPRESSION

Little Napoleons and Dummy Directors (1933)
Being the Narrative of the Bank of United States

The Barter Lady (1934)
A Woman Farmer Sees It Through

The House of Dawn (1935)
A Novel

WORLD WAR II

The Island (1944)
A History of the First Marine Division on Guadalcanal

Robinson Crusoe, USN (1945)
The Adventures of George R. Tweed Rm1c on Japanese-Held Guam

The Bismarck Episode (1948)

ROBINSON CRUSOE, USN

*The Adventures of George R. Tweed, R*M1C
on Japanese-Held Guam

GEORGE R. TWEED

As Told To
BLAKE CLARK

WESTHOLME
Yardley

Originally published in 1945 by Whittlesey House.

Westholme Publishing, LLC
904 Edgewood Road
Yardley, Pennsylvania 19067
Visit our Web site at www.westholmepublishing.com

First Printing: March 2010
10 9 8 7 6 5 4 3 2 1

ISBN: 978-1-59416-111-7

Printed in United States of America.

CONTENTS

DANIEL DEFOE would have admired George Ray Tweed, the American seaman whose ingenuity and self-reliance have caught the imagination of modern America as Robinson Crusoe's fascinated eighteenth century England. Defoe's hero was engaged almost solely in a struggle for survival against nature. Tweed's similar fight was complicated by the necessity of evading a band of killers relentlessly tracking him from hideout to hideout.

Crusoe and Tweed were most alike in their genius for contrivance, and Tweed doesn't suffer from comparison with his famous prototype. To construct his shelter and furniture, Crusoe brought from his ship planks and boards and a complete carpenter's chest of tools, in addition to two saws, an ax, "an abundance of hatchets," a hammer, nails, and several knives. Tweed built his equipment without benefit of nails, using only a handsaw, a machete, and a pocketknife. He went on to fashion, with crude materials, a lamp, a lantern, and an ingenious alarm system. At one time he had electric lights in a part of the country where not even the best homes enjoyed such luxury. He kept in repair an almost worn-out typewriter, on which he produced a one-page underground newspaper. He tore apart an apparently useless radio, put it together again, and brought in news from a station thousands of miles away.

Tweed was born with common sense. A roustabout life as lumberman, stevedore, and mechanic gave him self-reliance; hunting expeditions in Oregon and California taught him woodsmanship; the Navy instructed him in the techniques of communication. It was as if all his early life had been preparation for the grueling experience which he alone, of those who fled before the invading Japanese, survived.

I am glad to be the one to tell Tweed's story. In all important respects it is related here exactly as he gave it to me.

BLAKE CLARK

Washington, D. C.
December 21, 1944

PART ONE

THE CHASE

1

"DAMN Leathernecks!" I swore, as rifle and machine-gun fire penetrated my sleep. "You would come out here practicing and wake people up in the middle of the night!" It was three in the morning. I rolled over and went back to sleep.

Then I heard the field guns. First came the blast that sounded like a young cannon when the guns were fired, then the report of the exploding shell. That woke me up and snapped me out of it. We Americans had no field guns on Guam.

"That's not Marines! That's Jap fire!"

I scrambled up, knowing exactly what I wanted to do. At the Navy Communication Office where I worked as radioman we had discussed plans for action long before the first bomb fell on December 8. We knew that unfortified Guam could not hold out long. There were two choices, long argued about in bull sessions. We could take to the bush and hide out in the jungle where there was a good chance of not being discovered, or we could surrender and become prisoners of the Japs.

It was not a hard decision for me to make. I wasn't going

to be prodded in the rear with a bayonet by a Jap soldier.

As I pulled on my khaki shirt and trousers, Al Tyson rushed in with a Chamorro named Gevarra, who was in the insular service. Al was one of my best friends on Guam. He had made up his mind to go to the bush with me.

"For God's sake, hurry, Ray! Let's get out of here," he called. "The Japs are in!"

"We can't go without permission from headquarters," I yelled back at him. "I'm not going to be charged with running out under fire!"

"You can't cross the street to get an okay now," he said. "The Japs have a machine gun set up in front of the church."

"I'll have to go anyway. I've got to bust up those transmitters and generators before the Japs get them."

"I was just over there," Al said. "The men on watch smashed them. Come on. Let's get the hell out of here!"

"I still have to get authorization," I said stubbornly.

"I just *got* permission from the Governor's palace."

"Maybe you did, but that won't help *me* any."

"The commander said it was all right for us to take to the bush."

"Well, he didn't tell me that. I'll have to go over there," I said, and ducked out. Practically speaking, Al was right, but after eighteen years of Navy training my mind worked according to regulations.

My house was on a side street. It led into the main avenue, San Ramón. As I ran across, the Jap machine gunner started firing. I was about one hundred yards away from him, and he missed me. Once on the other side, I dove into a hedge, then over a fence, and made my way to the palace of the Governor, Capt. George J. McMillin. Inside I met Commander Giles, his aide. There was no excitement in his voice. He sounded as if he were discussing the attack over breakfast coffee.

"We are going to offer only token resistance and surrender," he told me. "We haven't enough men to fight it out. Do you have a gun?"

"No, sir, I haven't," I answered, hoping he might hand me one.

"Well, you can make your own decision. You can stay with us and surrender, or fend for yourself in the bush."

"Thank you, sir. That's all I wanted to know. I'll take the bush."

He shook hands with me and wished me luck. As I hurried out, I met Chief Yeoman Blaha, Yeoman Eads, and Chief Machinist's Mate Smoot. It flashed into my mind that Smoot two days ago had told me that he'd had a premonition he was going to be killed. He had worried himself sick about it.

"How're you doing, Smoot?" I asked.

"Okay," he answered. "We're going to the bush."

"See you there," I called over my shoulder and ran out the back way.

I dodged across the street again before the machine gunner could get a line on me, and found Al and Gevarra at home still waiting. The Jap field gun, which had ceased firing for a while, started up again, much closer. Poor Gevarra was frightened almost out of his senses. He picked up the cardboard back of a writing tablet lying on the table, crouched down in a corner and put the square of paper over his face for a shield. There was no use trying to buck him up. We had to work fast.

I rushed into the bedroom and yanked a pillow off the bed. Into the case I shoved two suits of underwear, a Navy issue blanket, and a flashlight. I threw the gear into an apple box filled with canned goods, the last order from the Navy Commissary. Just as I hoisted the provisions to leave, Al stopped me.

"It's too late, now. We can't go out there. We'll be killed."

"If we sit here, it's a cinch we'll be taken prisoner. Every second counts. If we're going, we've got to leave now."

We just couldn't waste time arguing. Gevarra was still hiding behind the piece of cardboard.

I ran into the street, flung the groceries in the back of the car, and jumped in behind the wheel. As I stepped on the starter, Al shot down the steps and climbed in beside me. Gevarra jumped into the back seat. As I raced down the street, I realized that as soon as I turned into San Ramón, where the machine gun was set up, we had to climb a very steep hill. I didn't want to stall on that hill. I was afraid to risk shifting gears. I thought that in the excitement I might get mixed up. So before we reached San Ramón, I put her in low gear and jammed that throttle down to the floor boards. The old jalopy sounded like a heavy ten-ton truck. It was a 1926 Reo, with a big six-cylinder engine, and it really let out a bellow. We roared around the corner and shot up the hill wide open. The machine gunner concentrated on us. He sent clip after clip stuttering our way. Bullets splattered all around us, hitting the street, the gravel, and the rocks. Gevarra hugged the floor boards. It was only about two hundred yards up the hill, but scuttling along in low gear, and hearing the staccato of Jap machine-gun bullets all around us, we thought it was a heluva long way.

I wasn't exactly scared at this point, but I was excited.

Speeding on that road demanded all my attention. I shifted into high when we reached the top of the hill. I had not turned on my headlights before, but now, racing along the narrow road in the dark, I switched them on. A few days before, when I'd had orders to paint them black, with just a tiny square left in the middle, I thought they would throw no light at all, but now that I didn't want to be seen they seemed like two Army searchlights streaming down the country road.

We got out as far as Gevarra's ranch. Between bullets I had decided it would be better for Tyson and me to go on by ourselves. I felt pretty sure that Gevarra would never be satisfied to stay hidden in the far bush as we would have to. I knew that if my family were near, as his was, I'd have to know what they were doing and how they were getting along. I stopped at the driveway. I hated to tell him we didn't want him.

"What are you going to do?" I asked. "Do you want to go out with us, or stay here at home?"

Gevarra was subject to being taken prisoner just as we were. He hesitated.

"Don't you think it would be better if you were with your family?" I asked.

"Yeah, I guess you're right," he replied slowly and climbed out. We wished him good luck and went on.

The first gray of morning was beginning to light up the little ranch houses on the small farms that we passed. We drove about ten miles, nearly to the town of Yoña. I turned off on a small dirt road, hoping to find a place to hide the car. When I had gone about one hundred feet, I found I was right in the yard of a ranch. The whole family ran out at the noise. Did I feel stupid! I didn't want it broad-

cast that Americans were on their way to the bush, but how
could I explain why I had driven up their private road? It
would look foolish to back out without saying anything, and
so I pretended I was out warning the natives and shouted,
"The Japs have come ashore! The Japs have landed!"

They screamed back, "They have?" I shifted into reverse.
As I backed out, Al said, "For cripes sake, Ray, isn't this
that Jap Sudo's ranch?" I felt sillier than ever! Here I
was warning these Japs that the Japs had come!

Racing past the town of Yoña, I wheeled right on another
dirt road. After going half a mile, we swerved left into an
open field, grown up with tall weeds, that led to a small hill.
Bouncing over boulders and skidding on loose dirt, we made
the crest. There below us was nothing but tangled underbrush. A perfect hiding place for the car! I shifted to
second and gunned her as hard as I could. Jerking forward,
she shot into the growth and practically buried herself in
the matted bushes. As the old Reo bogged down, we
jumped out. I took out the ignition key and with a pair of
pliers yanked out the distributor. I hid it deep in the
thicket and camouflaged the top of the car with leaves and
branches. I didn't want any Jap riding around in my car!

The apple box in which we had packed our supplies was
too cumbersome to drag through the brush. We emptied
it and divided the canned goods, throwing half into the
pillowcase for Al to carry. The rest we tossed into the
blanket, tied the corners together, and I slung it over my
shoulder.

Plunging into the thicket, we got our first real taste of
the bush of Guam. Its foundation is a devilish shrub that
goes by the disarming name of *lemonchina*, "China lemon."
"China swordsman" would have been more accurate. Chest

high and thickly matted together, it is covered with sharp thorns half an inch long. Nothing has checked this growth for hundreds of years, and it was only with the greatest difficulty that we found openings we could get through.

The old Reo was deep in the bushes.

We had gone only a short distance when the spiny thorns ripped open the pillowcase, and the food spilled out on the ground. In nervous haste, we loaded it all into the blanket and fought our way to a comparatively open space, planted with coconut trees.

Just as we reached the middle of this grove, we were alarmed to see a native woman coming toward us. It was too late for us to change our course—she had already seen us. What if she should report us and put a search party on our trail? Better to act as if there was nothing unusual in two American sailors stumbling through a coconut grove somewhere on Guam at daybreak. The woman's black hair shone in the sun, and she wore no stockings on her brown legs. As we passed, I cleared my throat, put on as natural a smile as I could, and said, "Good morning!" She nodded in a cheerful way and answered, "How d'ye do?" just as if it were ten o'clock on the main street in town. She seemed to think no more of seeing us than, "How nice to exchange a friendly greeting so early in the morning!"

We looked across the clearing and saw a solid wall of *lemonchina* lining the edge of a deep canyon.

"We ought to find a swell place to hide in there," I told Al. But once we were in the thicket, a hideout was harder to locate than we had bargained for. There were plenty of places deep enough in the bush for safety, but none were on level ground. We knew we couldn't lie down on the steep side of a hill and expect to get a good night's sleep. By the time we found a well-secluded flat site, it was early evening. We felt as if we had dragged that loaded blanket over half of Guam.

As we sank down on the ground in relief, I suddenly realized that we had forgotten the most important thing—water.

"Just a couple of tenderfeet!" I said bitterly.

"We passed a gasoline drum on the way up; maybe there's some rain water in that," Al suggested.

We were suddenly suffering from thirst now that we knew we had no way to quench it. Forgetting our aching muscles, we headed back down the hillside. In the drum was a foot of water—red with rust. Now the craving was worse than ever. We slowly climbed the path again.

"I hate to go into our food supplies," I said to Al, "but some of that soup would do the trick."

I took my knife and opened a can, being careful not to spill any of the contents. Al was at my elbow, eagerly looking on. I pushed up the top—it was *concentrated* soup, requiring a can of water to make it fit to eat! We dove in with our fingers, anyway, but the stock was heavily salted, in readiness for the water mixture. We were worse off than before.

Then, further up the side of the canyon I saw a lone coconut tree that immediately cheered us up. We made a beeline for it. If we could just get one of the coconuts, it would be filled with juice. With difficulty I climbed the slanting trunk and twisted off a heavy nut. I opened it with my pocketknife, one of our very few tools. The blade broke off in the tough shell. We divided the thin milk that trickled out. It was only a teaser. I climbed after another nut, opened it, and snapped off the other knife blade! The coconut water tasted good—very good—but the sweet liquid failed to satisfy our thirst. It was a poor exchange for two valuable knife blades.

Suddenly we heard a noise and anxiously peered through the bush.

"Look, Ray," Al whispered excitedly. "There's someone coming this way!"

I parted the *lemonchinas* and saw an old man approaching. He had on a khaki shirt and shorts and was tall for a native. His hair was gray, and he had a wrinkled Spanish-looking face. We didn't want anyone to know where we

were, but our thirst was growing each minute and would
get serious pretty soon. We hastily decided to stop him
and ask for water. That first day in the bush we were not
so cautious.

"Hello, friend!"

Confronted by two sailors unexpectedly coming out of
the middle of the bush, the old man was startled at first.
He was such an old-timer that he spoke no English, and our
Chamorro was pretty elementary, but I could say "*janom*"—
water.

Instantly he was all sympathy. He grinned and nodded
at us and climbed right up the coconut tree. With his
machete he sliced the noses off two green coconuts and presented them to us! We felt very grateful, but we let him
know that we still wanted "*janom*," and he motioned us to
come with him.

We followed a dim trail to his house, two rooms made
of rough boards, covered with a tin roof. An old lady sat
in the shade of a breadfruit tree, weaving thatch. Women
and children of all ages poured out of the house. A pretty
pug-nosed girl who said her name was Isabel spoke up and
told us that this was the Ogo family. She introduced Francisco, the old gentleman; his wife, the old lady; then his
daughter and his granddaughter. Francisco waved vaguely
at several smaller children, one of whom he sent off to the
concrete cistern for rainwater. Another disappeared into
the house and brought us two large dishes of boiled *gado,*
a root which tastes like a white sweet potato. Perhaps it's
not the most tasty food in the world, but we were ravenous,
and it hit the spot.

With Isabel acting as interpreter, we explained that the
Japs had taken Guam and our lives were in real danger.

Francisco, who was a patriotic native, offered us shelter in his home even though it made him our accomplice. He took us into the house, and his wife spread two clean mats on the floor and put spotless cases on the pillows.

We had hardly stretched out before we heard a deafening roar of motors on the highway. With the speed of lightning we reached a window and warily peered out. Not fifty feet away, Jap army trucks loaded with armed soldiers were passing by! At any minute one might turn into the yard. We were off to the jungle again! Francisco grabbed up mats and pillows and led us to the edge of the bush near his house. We crawled through a narrow opening and working as quickly and quietly as we could, cleaned off a space inside. Francisco brought cool, green coconut fronds and spread them on the ground. He put the woven mats on them and left, wishing us *Buenas noches* for our first night in the bush.

2

I COULDN'T sleep. I lay on the mat in the dark and thought of a thousand different things. I remembered the first day I saw the island of Guam from the deck of a Navy transport back in August, 1939. The island had looked green and fertile, as a South Sea island should. A steady trade wind bent the line of palm trees on the beach and whipped my trousers about my legs. The narrow white-sand beach circling the coastline seemed hardly able to hold back the tropical growth that spilled from the mountains and plateaus right down almost to the water's edge. There were no houses in view, nothing but green forest in the south and sweeping tableland in the north as far as I could see. Much of this land had probably never been set foot on, I had thought, plenty of room here for hikes and hunting.

The road that led from the landing to Agaña, the capital, ran close to the beach through coconut groves, past tidy little villages, straight to the Plaza de España in the center of town. It had been an unexpected pleasure to find a well-planned city here in the middle of the Pacific. It covered a mile east and west between the ocean and a sharp line of coral bluffs. As I had driven along smooth macadam streets named for famous Spanish generals and explorers, I had been surprised to see many automobiles, comfortable-looking concrete homes, and modern business houses and theaters. The old palace, now the Government House, the Naval Hospital, and the Catholic Church gave the town dignity and a general air of peace and prosperity. "Agaña can stand up to any city its size at home," I had decided.

As an old Navy man of sixteen years' standing, I'd done turns of duty at many other ports and islands, but I liked Guam best.

My family and I had been quartered in an up-to-date house with a refrigerator, telephone, electric lights, and all the conveniences we could have had anywhere. Pan American Clippers brought us mainland mail less than a week old, so that my folks in Portland, Oregon, did not seem to be 5,000 miles away.

I'd gone to work as matériel man at the Navy Communication Office, where all radio messages were sent and received. News of the world reached us first of all the people on Guam. It was my job to see that the valuable radio equipment was always in working order. It gave me considerable satisfaction to know that I had a part in keeping the 24,000 people on this island in constant contact with the rest of the world.

I liked the natives, the Chamorros, whom I saw on the streets and traded with in the stores. Their melodious speech was a dialect of Malay strongly influenced by Spanish and Philippine Talag. Practically everybody spoke English, as nearly three generations had had the benefit of American schools established in 1898, when the island came under United States control. The Chamorros were as a rule nice looking, smooth skinned, brown, and very healthy. Their fine health they owe, to a great degree, to Navy medical men who came in with modern methods of sanitation and practically wiped out dysentery and other tropical diseases. Most of the natives have mixed blood, Chamorro, Spanish, and Filipino, the basic stock coming from the Chamorros, who first settled Guam centuries ago. The men are short but well built, with strong, muscular legs. The women are small and graceful, with snapping dark eyes. Nearly all of them have beautiful black hair, and they love to sit in the sun and brush it for hours at a time. I soon saw that the Chamorros liked gaiety and good times. They chattered and made jokes and laughed and really enjoyed themselves.

As months passed, I didn't tire of Guam. One reason was that the island, shaped somewhat like a human foot, was quite a sizable area. Its 225 square miles made only a tiny speck on a map of the world, but didn't seem small once I was on it. Since Guam is entirely surrounded by water, I had the idea I might get a hemmed-in feeling after a few months. But it is thirty miles long and from four to eight miles across, and so I couldn't stand at any one place and see the ocean on all sides.

Often on week ends I'd hike over the ridge of wooded hills which cut the island in two at its narrowest part. The southern half is high and mountainous near the center and slopes into rolling hills some distance from the sea. This is good farming land and is planted in coconuts, corn, rice, and taro. There are villages of from 200 to 1,000 people every few miles. Northern Guam is entirely different. It is just one great plateau rising out of the sea 200 to 500 feet on all sides, and sloping inland. The highest cliffs are the farthest north. They are covered with jungle growth, and their bases are beaten constantly by the sea.

Knowing the island and its people as I did, I'd hoped that better preparations would have been made for their defense. We'd had several indications that war was on the way. The Jap civilian cabinet had fallen, and everybody knew that the army mob wanted to fight. The United States Navy had evacuated American women and children from Guam in October. Yet when I had run to the Communication Office at five o'clock on the morning that the first Jap bomb fell, on December 8, and asked what we were supposed to do, the only thing the Chief could say was, "I don't know." Everyone in the office realized that there was nothing we could do. Our force consisted of 155 Marines, 200 natives of the insular force, and 400 Navy personnel. The Navy men were all petty officers and specialists, untrained for combat. The largest guns on the island were about half a dozen .30 caliber machine guns. One was mounted on the hill above Agaña for defense against air attack, another went to the insular force, one to the civil jail, and the others to the Marines.

Shortly after noon on the same day, the Jap bombers had destroyed the telephone lines at Libugon Hill. I was sent out with a portable transmitter to maintain communications. I had hardly got there when the Jap planes came in again. A fighter headed for me, machine guns sputtering. I was in the middle of an open field, on a sloping hillside. All I could do was hit the dirt. My khaki work uniform blended with the dead grass. The Jap stopped shooting. He had lost sight of me.

I'd lain there, wondering whether I could make it across to cover in the bushes, but every time I looked up, I saw a

Jap scout diving and strafing. I hugged the ground, squint-
ing up at the sky. A Jap bomber came toward my hill.
While I watched, the bays opened and let go a 100-pound
bomb. I looked down underneath the plane, trying to find
the military objective. I could see none. Then I saw that
the bomb was careening with the plane in my direction, but
still I wasn't scared. I thought it would hit the ground
long before it reached me. It kept sailing. It seemed to
gain momentum. It was revolving, and every time it turned
it made a swishing sound.

The speed of the bomb became terrific as it got nearer.
It seemed to be making a beeline right for me. Through
my mind flashed the thought, "It's going to be tough to be
washed up on the first day of the war." The bomb grew
bigger and bigger. I froze to the ground. In the last possible second, it passed over me and struck the earth. I covered my head with my arms as it hit. The concussion
bounced me off the ground. My head felt as though it were
bursting. My ear drums ached as if long, slender needles
had pierced them both at the same time. My back and legs
felt as if they were on fire. Steel fragments had fallen on
me.

I tried again to run for cover, but the torture had only
just begun. More planes joined the first. I would look up,
thinking each bomb was going to hit me, and it would pass
over my head, landing fifty or seventy-five feet beyond.
Small hunks of red-hot metal continued to fall on me, burning through my clothes before I could brush them off. One
cut a deep gash in my hand. A heavy rock fell in the middle
of my back, and for a moment I thought my spine was
broken.

After an hour and twenty minutes the planes had wheeled

out to sea. The Japs had been poor shots. The bombs that almost got me had undoubtedly been aimed at a steel-tower airplane beacon, still untouched 100 feet up the hill. It was some grim satisfaction to know they were such lousy marksmen.

Back in Agaña, still shaking from the experience, I'd stopped in front of the Elks Club to go across the street for a drink. A native came up and spoke to me.

"Only one bomb fell on the city," he said.

"What did it hit?"

"Your house!"

"The hell you say!"

I raced home, and there it was, practically demolished. The first day of the war, the only bomb dropped in Agaña, and it had to hit my house! I didn't have to open the front door—it was blasted out. The living room was so full of dirt and debris that I couldn't climb in. I pulled out lumber and trash, throwing them into the yard so that I could enter.

The bomb had gone clear through the roof and exploded on the front porch. Four-inch concrete walls had saved the house from complete destruction. Even so, the roof had been blown off, and most of the ceiling boards were piled on the floors of the various rooms. One heavy plank was driven endwise through the top of the maple dining-room table, another through the foot of the bed. The bed-stead had literally exploded; springs and tufts of mattress were scattered all over the floor. The alarm clock had been slammed right through the closet door and had fallen to the floor inside. It looked as if it had been run over by a train.

I realized that I was terribly hungry and weak. I found some cold meat and made some sandwiches before reporting to the Communication Office. When I arrived, I found sledge hammers lying on the tables. We were to use them to wreck the radio transmitters and generators if the Japs came ashore.

"They say we're going to put up a fight," one of the men announced. "The Governor had instructions to surrender, but Colonel McNulty told him, 'No, the Marine Corps doesn't give up without a fight,' so the Governor agreed to putting up a token resistance."

We sure had to hand it to the Marines. At all costs they were going to uphold their tradition of honor.

Lying there on the mat beside Al in the darkness I wondered how the Marines were making out. Al was awake, too, and we talked about it. We decided the jig was probably about up in Agaña by now. We worried about what had happened to our friends. Which ones had surrendered to the Japs? Who else had taken to the bush? We discussed Eads's and Blaha's chances in the wilds. We mulled over Smoot's premonition.

I kept thinking that Chief Myers, my immediate superior in the radio repair shop, might be somewhere out here. He had often said that he would take to the hills in preference to the Japs anytime. I liked Myers. He was a swell fellow—easygoing, not excitable, taking everything in his stride when everybody else got their beards in a blaze. We were the best of friends, and I hoped that he'd make out okay whatever he'd finally done.

So far as we knew, we were the only two Americans who had made it out to the bush. Had we done right in striking off on our own? How soon would the American Navy recapture Guam? On this last point, we had heard a great deal of big talk. "I just came out from the states on a transport," some cocksure seaman would say, "and I saw American ships all over the Pacific on the way out here. If the Japs ever dare to attack Guam, in forty-eight hours the United States Navy will throw a ring of steel all around this island and blast them to pieces." We weren't completely taken in by such boasts, but we did believe that we wouldn't be stranded without military aid for very long.

Al and I decided that it would probably be a month to six weeks, taking everything into account—the size of the task force that would be needed, the time it would take to get it organized, and how soon it could plough in from San Francisco and Hawaii. Six weeks, we agreed, was a conservative estimate. If the Americans would be here by then, what was the use of surrendering? We could surely hold out that long.

Finally we settled down to try to get some sleep. Mosquitoes nearly ate us up. We took off our undershirts and wrapped them around our heads, leaving a tiny opening to breathe through, but, as soon as we dozed off, we'd lose the shirts and the mosquitoes were at us again. It was too warm for a blanket, but we pulled ours over us for protection. The little devils streamed in through a hole. We turned the blanket so that the hole was near the bottom, and then they bit our feet. We were not used to sleeping on the ground. The mat was quite thin, more like a plaited throw rug than a mattress. It was no protection against the small sticks and rocks in the hard ground beneath us. We twisted and turned, trying to avoid them, but only uncovered more rocks. After a few hours of this, our backs felt as if they had been beaten with clubs.

Worried as we were and unable to sleep, we were suspicious of any noise in the dark. Several times we heard what we were sure were heavy footsteps. We finally realized that it was one of the thousands of monstrous toads that inhabit Guam. They take several good-sized hops at a time, and each one sounds like a man's foot landing on the leaves. Again, we were sure we heard someone give a low whistle and call, "Kitty, kitty." After a lot of trouble, we located the sender and saw that it was a bird of some kind that I'd never seen before. Rats scampered through our little clearing. One started to chew my hair when I finally slept a little toward morning.

3

A T SUNUP Francisco came out to move us to a safer spot. We settled a quarter of a mile away—in a heavy clump of bushes about one hundred feet off a small trail. We cleared off a space on level ground and put down the mat. We covered the gallon jug of water that Francisco brought us with leaves to keep it cool and arranged our small store of canned goods in a shady niche where no sun's rays reflected from the tins could give away our hideout.

Francisco brought us a meal of green beans, fried eggs, and rice. I didn't really like the way the Chamorros cooked rice, very dry, each grain separate from every other. When we had rice in Oregon, we served it like a cereal—boiled soft—and we put milk and sugar on it. But right now rice à la Francisco was wonderful, and I wolfed it down. We didn't know how long we would be in the bush waiting for the United States Navy to retake Guam, and so we wanted to conserve our canned food. We were afraid that something might happen to drive us in deeper where we would have to look out for ourselves without help from any natives.

After two days I began to feel unsafe. We were only a short distance in the bushes bordering on an open field through which people sometimes passed to and from work. I didn't believe that any natives would report us, but I was afraid that they might gossip until word reached the Japs. We talked in low tones and tried to be very quiet, but it was easy to forget or to drop something that would make a lot of noise. We agreed to move further away.

With this idea in mind, that night, while Al held the fort at our shelter, I set out for the car to collect any useful tools I might salvage. We didn't even have a can opener since I had broken my pocketknife.

Finding the car was easier said than done. There was no moon, it was pitch black, and I couldn't see far enough ahead to get my bearings. I had to return emptyhanded to the hideout. This experience taught me how hard it was to reach any definite objective at night through the dense bush.

Next morning something happened to show me that Al was worse off than I was when it came to finding his way alone.

"I'll look for a better hiding place while you find out how to get to the car," Al suggested.

"Okay, we'll meet back here in half an hour."

We separated at the bottom of the canyon. I followed the trail to the edge of the clearing and peeked out to see how I had fouled up the night before. I got my bearings and believed I could make it now in the dark.

Half an hour had passed when I reached the hideout, but Al wasn't there. After waiting nearly two hours, I crept to the edge of the canyon and cautiously looked around. There in an open field not a hundred yards from the main road used by the Japs, I saw Al. He was hopelessly lost, going around the edge of the field trying to find the entrance to our hideout. I was afraid he might head for the road and run into some Japs. I whistled and he came in, but three Chamorros at work in a cornfield saw him.

So then I realized that Al, like many people, had no sense of direction, and I'd have to look out for him. The reason I could make my way was that I had lived in the hills of southern Oregon for four years when I was a boy. I had had a .22 rifle and ranged the country with it. Starting in the early morning and staying out all day, I'd often go as far as ten miles away from home at a time. I developed a good memory for landmarks. In later years, while living in San Diego, four of us had got licenses each season to hunt deer in the mountains. These expeditions gave me refresher courses in woodsmanship. I have never been lost in the woods. I have strayed off trails but have always been sure of my direction.

We thought that the natives who saw Al would tell their families about it, and so we decided not to stick around there another night. While Al waited, I went down into the canyon and up the hill on the other side, looking for a suitable place. I found a good one—a clump of *lemonchina* on level ground under a big tree. I figured that the tree would shield us from Jap planes, and the bushes were so thick that I had to crawl on my hands and knees to get into them—a good hiding place, for sure.

So we moved, lugging with us a large piece of corrugated tin roofing which Francisco had given us. We couldn't get in touch with Francisco without approaching his house, which we didn't want to do. This meant that we had to make inroads on our supply of canned goods. We had

about thirty cans, mostly corn, peas, pork and beans, some
corned beef, and one very handsome can of brown bread. It
was the largest can we had, and it had been the only one of
its kind in the commissary. We often said, "I'll bet that's
good; let's eat it later on," and decided to save it a little
longer. We agreed to ration ourselves to one can a day
each. It was a strict regimen and damned hard to keep.
By the third day we were about to break it when something more serious claimed our attention. We ran out of
water.

We had no idea where to fill our jug. We were learning
to our sorrow that the greatest difficulty in living off the
land in Guam was the scarcity of streams or springs.

"We'll have to contact Francisco again," Al said.

We took turns sitting at the bottom of the hill, watching
the trail which led to his cow pasture. It was not until
two days later, when our throats were parched, that Al saw
him and brought him in.

At seeing us again, the old man grinned with pleasure,
showing his discolored teeth.

"*Bueno, bueno!*" He pointed to our tin roof, covered
with branches to prevent a reflection which might attract
Jap planes.

"*Muy bien!*" he exclaimed, his approval caught this time
by the way we had tied five cartons of cigarettes underneath the tin to keep them dry in case of rain.

Francisco nodded vigorously when we said, "*janom,*" in-
dicating that he would be very glad to bring us some. He
went off and came back carrying food as well as water.

Preparing to stay, we made our cramped quarters more
livable. About fifteen feet from our shelter we cleared out
enough bushes so that we could stand upright. Then we

cleared a trail to the outside so that we could go out or come in by crouching or stooping instead of crawling on our hands and knees. We had no visibility greater than a few feet unless we went outside where we could look across the canyon.

On Francisco's next visit he brought a neighbor, a tanned countryman of forty, named Juan Cruz. He wore blue dungarees, a blue denim shirt open at the neck, and a gray felt hat pulled well down over his eyes. He explained that Francisco had told him about us and he wanted to help. I thought I'd better test him with a few questions.

"Why are you willing to risk helping us? If the Japs find out, they'll put you in jail."

"I'll take a chance," he replied. "I don't like Japs. If I can help Americans, that's what I want to do."

"Why do you like Americans better than Japs?"

"Who wouldn't?" he laughed. "Before sometimes we used to see Chamorros from Saipan. Japs treat 'em like dirt. Saipan Chamorro is always poor—Japs take his eggs, milk, anything. He can't get good job in town. Nothing."

"Don't you think the Japs might be here to stay?"

He laughed again, showing strong white teeth. "Just look at Jap man, then look at American man," he observed. "American will win."

Something about Juan—his direct, honest manner, and the way he smiled all the time—convinced me that he was a solid citizen who could be depended upon in a tight spot. I was glad he had come.

Francisco brought us food one morning, Juan brought it the next. We tried to set aside some for our other meals, but in an hour it would be alive with ants. I made a "board" of slender sticks cut from bushes and tied together with vines. We suspended the board from the branch of a tree, making a shelf in mid-air. "The ants might smell the food up there but they won't have sense enough to crawl up the tree and down the vines to get it," we figured. This worked for a couple of days until some ant strayed down the vine, found the feast, and went back for his friends and relatives. Then we had to transfer our pantry to another tree.

When we spread our chow out on the mat and sat down to eat, flies swarmed in. Lizards came to catch them. These lizards were harmless and plentiful—young ones with bright-blue tails and older ones five inches long with quick bright eyes and darting tongues. They climbed up on our arms and shoulders and stuffed themselves on the pests buzzing about our ears.

After some days of this squatting on the ground, I decided to build a table. With a machete Francisco brought me, I chopped down some small trees and cut four poles about four inches in diameter for table legs. I notched them, stood them up, and connected them by fitting long slender poles into the notches. This made a topless framework. Then I cut several of the soft roots of the *kaful* tree. These branch out from the trunk of the tree on all sides like an upside-down bowl. I split some into boards three-quarters of an inch thick and four feet long and tied them with heavy vines to the framework to make the tabletop. The rough wood made my hands raw, and the tough vines raised huge water blisters, but I was so eager to see the table finished that I stopped for nothing. The job took four days.

Having to stand up to eat from the table drove us to work on chairs. We cut small straight rounds from tree branches and notched and fitted them together for the framework. I wove vines tautly back and forth across the framework

for a seat. Al did the same, using the streamers of coconut fronds instead of vines. Now we sat at table and ate
in style.

As the days passed, Al and I got dirtier and dirtier. Our
hair grew bushy at the temples, and climbed down the
backs of our necks, shaggy and matted. We kidded each
other about our beards. Al's was thin, mostly side burns
and goatee, and quite red. Mine was just a formless mass
of brush. My mustache hung down in front of my mouth
and got in everything I tried to eat or drink.

We had not had a bath in nearly five weeks, and we
smelled to high heaven. As we lay there on our mat, side
by side, I would say, "Al, you smell bad."

"I know, Ray. Confidentially, you stink!"

One afternoon it rained. Al jumped up and started pulling off his clothes. "I'm going to have a rainwater shower,"
he shouted. We had half a dozen bars of soap that had
happened to be in the commissary order and that we had
lugged around with us ever since. Al grabbed up one of
these virgin bars, stepped out into the shower, and began
soaping himself generously. Before he had finished, the
rain stopped as suddenly as it had begun, the sun came
out, and he was caught with a heavy lather all over his
body. We had one clean undershirt which we used as a dish
towel and one not so clean for our face towel. He grabbed
up the face towel and rubbed off part of the sticky mess,
but he had done too good a job. We sat around for hours
picking off gluey soap flakes from his itching body.

When Juan brought us our next meal, he said, "Mr.
Tweed, you're a radioman; do you know Jesús Quitugua?"

"Sus Quitugua? Sure, we know him well." Sus worked
at the Communication Office delivering *The Guam Eagle*,

the daily mimeographed newspaper that was run off there. He was about twenty-six, good-natured, and likable. An excellent cook, he used to be chef when we had special dinners at the Elks Club. He was also a born gossip and always had the latest news about everything going on on the island.

"I can bring him here if you'd like to see him," said Juan.

"Swell! Sus'll have all the dope."

"Okay, I'll bring him up tomorrow."

We were eagerly waiting when we heard the two coming through the bushes to our shelter.

"Tweed! The Japs want you bad!" Sus exclaimed when greetings were over. He went on to tell us about the trouble the Japs were having setting up radio communication with Japan. "They don't savvy how to fix the smashed transmitters and generators. They found a list in headquarters and saw your name, 'George R. Tweed, radio matériel man.' Right away they go to the church where the prisoners are locked up. They shout out, 'George R. Tweed.' No answer. They ask, 'Where's Tweed?' Nobody can tell 'em. So they know you're hiding out."

Four other Americans had escaped, too, Sus said. He didn't know their names, but two were chiefs. There had been more, but they had given themselves up and were now in prison.

"The Japs give reward for escaped Americans," continued Sus. "Ten yen for any American, fifty yen for radioman. They're afraid you're building a transmitter to communicate with the United States."

"God, don't I wish I could!" I exclaimed.

"They put up a notice about you in lots of places," Sus went on. "One in front of Pedro Martinez' store. Everybody was standing there staring at it and saying that was a good-sized reward when Pedro came out and read it. He turned around and told them, 'If any of you men need that money, come to me and I'll give you the fifty yen. Don't go hunting down an American for it.'"

It looked to me as if the Japs were going to have a hard time converting people as loyal as Pedro.

"The Japs are hunting for you all over the island, district by district," Sus warned. "They mean business—you'd better watch out."

Al and I looked at each other. So the Japs had a price on our heads already! We had rather hoped to lie low and not be missed, but they even had our names.

"What's happened to the other Americans, Sus? Where's Myers?"

"I haven't heard anything of him at all."

"What about Smoot?"

"Oh, you don't know about Smoot?" he asked with surprise, forgetting that he was telling us every word we had heard since December 10.

It was a sad story. When Smoot, Eads, and Blaha started to leave the Governor's palace by the back exit, their way was blocked by Japs. They whirled, ran out the front door, and through the Palace grounds. Halfway across, a Jap machine gun opened up on them. Eads fell flat on his face without being hit. He was later taken prisoner right there. Joe Blaha was shot in the pelvis and spine and went down. Smoot was hit, too, and he went down. The Japs came up and bayoneted Blaha as he lay wounded. Smoot went crazy. He pulled out his .45 and started picking them off. He killed eight or ten before a Jap officer unsheathed his

sword, sneaked up behind the fighting American and beheaded him.

We sat quietly, thinking about Smoot. He had plenty
of courage.

"Did you hear about Shinohara?" Sus asked.

"If you don't quit asking if we've heard something—!" Al
threatened.

"He was a Jap spy!"

"So that's why he was always trying to hobnob with
United States Navy big shots!" Al exclaimed.

Shinohara, owner of a big general merchandising store,
was one of the most prominent Japs on prewar Guam. He
made it a point to be especially polite to Navy officers, was
always trying to get them to come to colorful Japanese tea
parties and sukiyaki suppers.

"He sent information to Japan all the time," Sus claimed,
and went on to tell us that Jap troops landing on Guam
had more copies of our "confidential" maps of the island
than they knew how to read. I remembered bitterly how
we had kept those maps under lock and key.

"Shimizu was a spy, too—and Mrs. Sawada," Sus continued.

They too were merchants who made yearly "buying trips"
to Japan.

"Shimizu had a secret radio and sent out messages to
Jap ships off the island before the attack. They all three
got big rewards. They're numbers one, two, and three Jap
civilians on Guam, now. They spend most of their time in
meetings with Jap high officials. The officers gave Shinohara and Shimizu everything in the commissary, and they
moved it into their own stores to sell. Mrs. Sawada got the
building where the American Service Club used to be and

the Masonic Temple across the street. She's made them into recreation halls for Japs, charges for everything, and they let her keep all the money she makes—which is plenty!"

Then Sus told us how the Japs were mistreating the townspeople, running them out of their homes and grabbing all their goods. T. T. Calvo was whipped in public because he took some food out of his own general merchandise store for his hungry family.

Another thing that got my goat was that Jap sentries— lousy little runts who had lived hardly better than animals —made Chamorros stop and bow very low three or four times before letting them pass. Sometimes another Jap would walk behind the bent-over native and kick him in the rear so that he'd fall on his face. Then the damn Japs would laugh.

A neighbor of Sus's walked ten miles into town to the bakery and bought eight loaves of bread for his family. On the way back he passed a Jap sentry who took four loaves away from him. A couple of miles farther on, a second sentry grabbed the other four. The poor guy had walked twenty miles and spent his hard-earned cash to feed Japs.

It burned me up that the gentle Chamorros were being treated this way. Still there wasn't a thing I could do but sit there and cuss. I'd never been so frustrated in my life.

When Sus left, we lay back on our mats, talking over all the news he had brought. Those damn Japs! They'd pay for their cruelty when the United States took over again. We speculated about the other four Americans who had escaped to the bush. Who were they? Where were they hiding? Would we run into them?

4

A WEEK passed. Juan faithfully continued to bring us his share of food. One day while sitting with us in the sun, he suggested that we move to a shelter on the other side of the canyon, nearer his ranch.

"It'll be easier to come see you there. We'll keep it secret." His brown eyes flashed. "We won't tell even Francisco."

"If we leave here without letting him know, how will we get supplies?"

"Don't worry about that. Sus will feed you one day, me the next."

This sounded good to me. I liked Juan. He was easy to get along with. I'd never seen him angry. Better still, he knew how to handle himself in the bush. When the ordinary person goes through *lemonchina,* you can hear him a hundred yards away. Juan could come right up to our hideout without cracking a single twig. If we got in a jam, he'd be invaluable to us. We moved.

Our new home was practically the Waldorf-Astoria compared to the tin-roofed clearing we'd been in. It was a shelter, dug out of the hillside, the excavated dirt serving as a fill, making a level floor about five by twelve feet. This was covered by clean mats. A large piece of canvas stretched over it all made a good roof. Even further luxury was in store for us, because at night, Sus moved his unprotesting family of four up to Juan's and let us sleep comfortably at his house.

Juan had built this shelter to be used by his family as a hideout when the Japs invaded Guam.

"You fixed a mighty swanky place," I said. "How much of a family do you have, Juan?"

"Thirteen children," he replied. "Need plenty of room."

"Thirteen is an unlucky number," I teased him. "Better make it fourteen."

"Never mind," he smiled.

A few weeks later Juan announced the arrival of another little Cruz.

We lived a seemingly unreal existence. Days passed. The life of the island continued, but we were nonparticipants. We contributed nothing, had nothing to take satisfaction in except the fact that we were not yet caught. Sus brought us a deck of playing cards. For hours at a time we sat and played cooncan, rummy, and a game Al knew called "battle." Sus brought each of us a new pocketknife, and we passed a lot of time whittling soft wood. Sometimes, for pastime, we pretended that this was just a dream, that the Americans had not lost Guam, after all, and that there was really no need for us to hide. One day while we were sitting crosslegged, like a pair of Gandhis, staring out across the canyon, Al said, "Boy, wouldn't we feel like a couple of dopes if the Japs weren't really on Guam and we were wasting our lives out here in the bush for nothing?"

"Yeah," I agreed. "We'd just have to tell people we came

up here because we liked the scenery and the quietness, that we took to the bush because we didn't want to be bothered."

We were famished for news of the world. Sus said that the Japs were reporting terrific gains throughout the Pacific from Java to California. We didn't believe it, but we were anxious to hear something from the United States.

"Juan, can't you please get me a radio," I begged him practically every day after we got settled. "Any kind, any condition. You just bring it; I'll make the son-of-a-gun work."

About three weeks after I started plaguing him, Juan came in proudly bearing a rusty, patched-up box of tubes and wires. It looked like a repairman's nightmare.

"Here you are," he announced, "a radio!"

When I first looked at it, I had little hope of ever putting it in shape. However, after working over it for a considerable time, I brought it near enough to operation that, with a pair of headphones, I could hear the receiver oscillating. But I couldn't get any station on it. We rigged up a long piece of wire and stretched it between two coconut trees for an aerial but still couldn't bring anything in.

"This is no good. This pile of junk is just too far gone. We've got to have a real radio," I told Juan.

That was no small order. The Japs had forced everyone on the island who had a set to turn it in. They threatened that anyone caught with any kind of a receiver would have his head cut off. In Jap-held Guam, radios were rare as angels' voices.

Then one afternoon Juan walked in with a real radio. I recognized it as soon as I saw it as an old Silvertone that had belonged to Chief Aerographer Jones. Before the war

he'd brought it in for me to repair. It had needed a special
kind of tube that we didn't have on the island, and so Jones
had bought a new set and gave the old one to a native.

The Silvertone operated on both alternating and direct
current. It had two tubes that required twenty-five volts
for the filament. I knew that I'd have to replace these
tubes with one or two audio amplifiers requiring six volts
or less on the filaments to enable me to heat the filaments
from a car battery. Juan brought me the two dry-cell batteries I'd left in the car. These were for operating portable
transceivers and had various plate and filament voltages.
The highest plate voltage was 156, which I felt would be
sufficient for the plates.

The only tube I was able to obtain that would be suitable for an audio amplifier was a 2A5, using only two volts
on the filament. This required a separate heater circuit.
Juan brought me a soldering iron, solder, acid, and hook-up
wire that he'd got in town. I was so glad to see them, I
didn't even ask him where he'd found them. I heated the
iron in the fire and went to work. I built in sockets for the
tubes and rearranged the circuit to accommodate them.

In my shop, I'd have whipped this job into shape in a
morning. But heating the electric soldering iron over an
open fire of wood so wet it would hardly burn, working
outdoors where the breeze quickly dissipated the small
amount of heat I was able to get into the iron, struggling
with unsuitable and insufficient hook-up wire and incorrect
replacement parts, it took me days to do a job that should
have required only hours.

This was progress but not perfection. Programs would
come in, but we nearly went crazy because they were so
faint. It was hell to be able to catch the rise and fall of a

newscaster's voice and not be able to bring it in loud enough
to understand what he was saying. I racked my brain to
think of a way to increase the volume with the sketchy
materials I had on hand.

While I worked on the radio and Al played solitaire, Juan
and Sus continued to bring us food and local news. Lately,
the food was the better of the two. Every once in a while
Sus made pancakes that would just melt in our mouths.
I'll never forget them. Every time we had them, I asked
him for the recipe, but he never got around to giving it
to me.

The news was something else again. The Japs had developed a systematic method of searching for us. Section
after section was to be sieved until we were found. The
Commissioner of each district chosen was ordered to sum-
mon 200 to 400 men. These were given detailed instructions for flailing the bushes so thoroughly that no living
thing could escape. Armed Jap sailors and Saipan native
police supervised, being held personally responsible for seeing that the natives did a thorough job.

For the past several days the Japs had been covering our
district, and Juan himself had been forced to participate in
the hunt. He searched for us all day, then brought us
food at night. He reported to us what territory had been
"cleared" according to the Jap leader and on the attitude
of the Chamorros to the forced labor.

"My friends don't want to find you," he comforted us.
"They hear you Americans have guns. They think it's better to look the other way if they see a pistol."

"Good," we said.

"And," Juan continued, "it's easier to stay on the little
trail. Nobody's dumb enough to want to push their way

through the *lemonchina* stickers. They all know they'll
have to crawl through them on their stomachs if they're
gonna find you," he ended reassuringly.

After three or four weeks, however, the natives tired.
I realized what their frame of mind must be. They didn't
want to find the Americans, but they were fed up with
tramping through the bush every day, with no time off to
take care of their farms and animals. I thought how tough
it was on Juan. He had to neglect the crops that were to
provide food for his large family and yet come back at night
and feed us. Meantime, all we could do was sit there hour
after hour, fooling with the radio and unsuccessfully hiding
our nervousness with endless card games.

It was early in February when our routine was suddenly
interrupted. About nine o'clock one evening, Juan came
running in.

"You've got to beat it," he told us excitedly. "The search
party comes here in the morning!"

"My God! Are you sure?" we both shouted at once, jumping up.

"Ramón Baza was just here. He's the leader. He told
me, 'Get those Americans out of there! We search that district early tomorrow morning.'"

Hurriedly we threw together two bundles of canned
goods to take with us and hid the rest of our gear in the
bush. As we worked, we worried. Why had the Japs suddenly concentrated on this very ranch? Had someone reported us in hopes of collecting the reward? Packing in the
dark, I was afraid we might have left something behind.

"Juan, please come out here at daylight and be sure that
we haven't left anything lying around," I requested.

"Okay. Now, let's go! I've found out where the other

Americans are and fixed it up with the man who helps them. He'll take care of you until this blows over."

Good old Juan! He was a real friend. I'd lived in Guam two and a half years, but I'd learned more about its people in the past two months than in all that time. Now I saw what warm-hearted, brave, and, above all, loyal people they were. Juan knew that the Japs would torture or kill him if he were discovered helping us, yet he never hesitated.

The others were at Manengon, about three miles away across rough trails, a swamp, and the Ylig River. Juan led the way. Sus carried a third bag for us. When we reached the swamp, Juan warned us to tighten our shoe laces before we plunged in. He knew a trail across, but in the black night it was easy to step off into the oozy mud. When we did, we sank down halfway to our knees and the suction almost pulled our shoes off as we lifted our feet out.

We forded the Ylig River and climbed the pitch-dark trail to Manuel Aguon's.

"Be careful. Don't go too near," Juan warned us. "Manuel will fire his shotgun first, and ask questions afterwards!"

Juan tactfully called out about a hundred feet from the house, and Manuel strode to meet us. He was a stocky, muscular Chamorro, about thirty-five, who looked as though he could take care of himself and half a dozen others as well.

"Glad to have you Americans," he declared, shaking hands vigorously. "Manuel Aguon will help you out as long as you need him."

This was a warm welcome, and Manuel sounded as if he meant every word of it. He was a man after our own hearts. He was so prudent that he had never permitted even his own flesh and blood to know where he had hidden the Americans. When we set out, he told his brother Vicente we were going to an entirely different hill from the one to which he guided us. Al and I followed him briskly, excited at the idea of meeting the other Americans. In whispers we discussed who they might be. I hoped that one of them would be Myers.

Shortly after we reached level ground at the top of the mountain, we made out the outlines of a shelter. We saw no light, but smelled the smoke of a fire. As we drew near, we saw two men on guard a few feet outside the refuge.

"Manuel?" one of them called softly, and Manuel answered. It was so dark we had to peer into each other's faces. The first man I met was Johnston, a husky machinist's mate, first class, who had been attached to the minesweeper, *U.S.S. Penguin.* He grinned through a bushy beard and made us welcome. The others came out. I searched each face hopefully, but Meyers wasn't among them. They were Yeoman First Class Yablonsky, Chief Aerographer Jones, and Chief Machinist's Mate Krump. I knew them all. Yablonsky, or Ski as we called him, had come to Guam and started to work in the Communication Office a couple of months ago. He had a sharp, active mind and held his own on almost any subject in the office bull sessions. Everybody knew "Weatherman Jones," the lanky aerographer. He had come in for plenty of kidding every day at the office when he posted his forecast. We used to check every point—high and low temperature and amount of rainfall—and ride him about "his" weather.

We started to talk. "Sh-sh-sh! Everybody inside," Krump ordered. He was the leader, and looked the part. Tall and broad, he was physically the most rugged of the four. He happened to have senior rating among them, but

in our situation that would have made little difference had
he lacked the more vital qualifications.

We stooped to enter their shelter, which was hardly big
enough for the men's mat. It was just a rude pup tent, its
sloping sides formed by *agag* mats laid loosely across a
single ridge pole. Once inside, we had to sit down immediately; there was no room to stand upright. The fire took
up considerable space. It was laid on blocks built up about
two feet off the ground and had to be kept burning constantly to drive out the mosquitoes. The high bed of hardwood ashes showed that the men had been here for a good
while.

Al and I spoke in lowered voices, as we usually did, but
Krump silenced us. "Up here, we whisper," he warned.

We made a strange picture, the six of us, long haired and
bearded, squatting in the dim firelight. All of us wore
dirty khaki trousers and shirts. Jones and Krump still wore
their chief's caps, which now sat on top of their heads, unable to fit down over their bushy hair.

Far from being nervous or depressed, everyone was in
excellent spirits, and we talked excitedly, catching up on
what had happened since December 10. Jones said they
had counted on getting out of town in Smoot's car, but
when he failed to show up they set out on foot. I told them
that we got away in my old Reo.

"Then it was you who shot past us on the hill!" Ski said.
"We heard that thing gunning up San Ramón like a truck
full of Japs and jumped off the road into the bushes. Then
we saw it was your car. We yelled, but you didn't hear us."

"I wish to God we had. A little company right at that
time would have done our nerves some good," said Al.

"We had one piece of luck. We made it to an abandoned

chicken ranch in the mountains where we could forage for food. We were about to stay overnight in the empty house, but thought better of it and pushed on. A few minutes later we heard a roar, looked back, and saw three carloads of Jap soldiers pulling up into the ranch yard!"

"Some rabbit's foot you carry!" Tyson whistled.

The men went on with their story. In the days of wandering in the mountains and fighting for existence in the bush, Krump had proved to be best in ferreting out passage through the thickets and in finding safe sleeping places. I had to hand it to Krump.

"Our rabbit's foot was working best," he said, "the day we were taken in by Manuel Aguon." The others nodded. "He doesn't let on to a soul that he knows a thing about us. He guards this hideaway like a mother hen with a prize brood."

"Smart guy, Manuel," Johnston put in. "He's strictly a rancher—grows all kinds of vegetables, has lots of coconut and banana trees, and raises almost everything he needs for his family. All Manuel ever goes to the store for is sugar."

When we got around to the war, they too had it all worked out mathematically and figured it could not take longer than six to eight weeks for Guam to be safely back in American hands.

"We've got a better than fifty-fifty chance of holding out until the Navy gets here," I said. "For one thing, our experience with the natives shows they are all on our side. The more they see of the Japs, the more anxious they'll be to help us. The Chamorros are one hundred per cent American as far as I can tell. Except for the danger of their gossiping, I'd feel as safe in going to a native's house and

asking him to help me as if I were in Oregon asking my
next-door neighbor to hide me from Jap invaders."

"They do talk too damned much," Ski said.

"They sure do," agreed Krump, "and it may be we'll have
to break with them entirely some time and forage for ourselves. I'd hate like hell to do it, but I believe we could live
off the land long enough for the Navy to steam in."

"We can do it here if it can be done anywhere in the
world," Jones put in. "The climate is swell. Even if we
have to sleep outdoors we'll never freeze. The land's so
damn fertile it's indecent—you can eat practically everything
that grows here. Why, a man could live on *gado* alone if
he had to. Even these ungodly *lemonchina* bushes have red
berries that don't taste too bad."

"And nothing's poisonous—that's the best thing about it,"
Johnston added. "God, how would you like to try to live in
the jungle in New Guinea or some lousy place like that
where everything you touch can kill you—plants, snakes—
even the mosquitoes. These little bastards here may keep
us awake all night, but at least we know they don't give us
malaria or anything else."

"Yeah, it can be done all right," Krump summed it up.
"And, much as I hate 'em, these bushes will do more for us
than everything else. I'll bet there's fifty square miles of
lemonchina on this island. Before the Japs get me, they've
got to chase me all over that fifty square miles on their
hands and knees!"

"You said it, Mike!" Ski echoed the feelings of us all.

"Take Smoot," Krump went on. "I'm as sorry as I can
be about what happened to the poor guy, but that doesn't
keep us from learning a lesson from him. I think his premonition may have had something to do with his death. Out

here, we can't give in to pessimism. We've got to believe that everything is going to come out all right."

When we finally quit whispering and crawled to our crowded mats, our morale was high. Each of us believed that he had an excellent chance to come through alive.

5

THE next day we took turns standing guard on the cliff overlooking the valley. From there we could see the coconut groves and the river some eight hundred feet below, so that if a searching party crossed into our territory we'd be warned of its approach well ahead of time. It was Ski's shift, and while he was on watch he repeated to himself a list of Chamorro words that Manuel had given him. Ski was determined to make his forced exile in the bush count for something. "I'll be a high-class lingoist before this damn war is over!" he'd say.

About eleven o'clock Ski raced back from his post. "The Japs are fording the river!" he cried hoarsely. "About two hundred of them!"

We were excited, but we had tried to prepare for this emergency. Each man knew his place in the plan of action. We were to spread out from the shelter as if following the spokes of a wheel, and wait silently in the undergrowth. When the searchers reached the top of the hill, we'd have them surrounded. At a signal, we'd charge. Every Jap or Saipanese was to be killed, but we were not to harm any natives of Guam.

Since we were only six men and had only three pistols among us, our plan was ambitious, but we believed it would work. We felt we had nothing to fear from the Chamorros, and almost welcomed the chance to shoot it out with the half a dozen or so Japs who might be leading.

Johnston gave me his pistol, as he had never fired one, and in fact had difficulty in loading the clip. Ski went back to his lookout post on the cliff, and the rest of us took our positions. I was stationed near the trail. I was to let the searchers pass, and when the last man had gone by, rise up behind him to block their retreat.

We settled down to a period of nerve-wracking waiting. For six hours we crouched motionless in the thicket until every muscle ached. At last Ski crept to each man in turn and reported. "Okay, relax. They aren't coming up our side of the hill. They've just gone back across the river."

We gave sighs of relief and trekked back to the shelter. As we lit cigarettes Manuel quietly entered, perspiration standing out on his dark forehead. He had passed a horrible day as part of the search party that had come so close to finding us. "Every minute I was scared somebody'd see you. My heart was pounding all day." He wiped his brow. "You must leave *pronto*—tonight! Tomorrow morning we search this side of the hill!"

"Call the van, boys, here it is moving day again!" came from Jones. We were beginning to resign ourselves to constantly jumping from hillside to valley to bush.

We broke camp, destroyed all traces of the fire, buried every article left behind, and followed Manuel and Krump across the canyon through bush so thick that much of the way we were forced to crawl on hands and knees. Watch-

ing Jones, his six feet two doubled awkwardly as he labored
through the matted jungle, I was thankful I was short.

At last we reached the top of the hill. "This is a good
place," Manuel suggested. All of us were breathing hard
and were glad to arrive finally at a spot that he approved.
We crawled into the heart of a large clump of *lemonchina*
and began to clear a sleeping place.

"This ground is shallow—let's pull up these bushes by the
roots so we can put 'em back later and it won't show we've
been here," ordered Krump.

We fell asleep amid the *lemonchinas*, their exposed roots
looking like underfed parsnips in the dim night.

In the morning we replanted the bushes, stamping and
smoothing the ground so that no one walking by could have
told that the place had been disturbed. We took our bags
to a thick clump of bush near by and made that our headquarters for the day. Discussing our chances of dodging
the search party, no one ever once raised his voice above a
whisper. The others took cat naps, but I was never one to
sleep in the daytime. I had the deck of cards and played
cooncan with Johnston.

In the afternoon Krump and I took our machetes and dug
a few *gados*. As the season was late, most of them were
dried up, but we got a few good ones. We gave these to
Manuel to take home and cook for us when he came up
with food at nightfall.

All we had for breakfast the next day was one coconut
and two small oranges which we divided among the six of
us. We saved two thin slices of coconut apiece for lunch.
After this scanty meal we busied ourselves with our gear,
making repairs or repacking it so that it would be easier to
carry. I took seven dollars, all the money I had, from my

pocket, folded it into a small pellet, opened a seam about an inch long in my shirt collar, and shoved the wad inside. I knew it was officially worthless on Guam, but Sus had said it had black-market value, and anyway I thought I would be spending it at the Elks bar in about six weeks.

Lanky Jones, the aerographer, had just taken a piece of khaki cloth out of his bag to patch a rip in his shirt when we heard a crashing of dry branches and a native burst in on us.

"Get out, quick! Search party's on the way up! I'm with them!"

It was Manuel's brother, Vicente.

"Pack up everybody! Scram!" Krump ordered, but the order wasn't necessary. Every one of us had frantically grabbed up his gear and was already on the way.

Vicente ran ahead, leading us to a spacious field covered with high sword grass. "I can't stay away any longer. If the Japs get suspicious, they'll cut off my head," he whispered. "Keep going. Don't stop until you're miles back in the hills, and we won't find you!" He turned and shot down the steep slope.

As we pushed ahead on the double, Ski brought up the rear, carefully covering our flight. He picked up any leaves we broke from trees or shrubs and stuffed them into his pockets. He brushed out footprints and fluffed up leaves over them, hiding our trail.

After going about half a mile, we came upon a tangled mass of *lemonchina*, shot through with vicious *gado* vines. These sweet-potatolike plants send out roots from which tough thorns half to three-quarters of an inch long stick up and carpet the earth. "If we can just burrow into that, we ought to be safe," said Krump. "I can't see any native knocking himself out looking for us inside that mess."

I ran grim interference, carefully parting the jungle growth so that I could take a step without breaking or mashing down the vines. Finally we reached underbrush so thick we had to crawl to penetrate it. *Gado* thorns drew blood, but we didn't dare cry out. We painfully made our way, hoping the searching party would miss our trail.

Then we heard them coming—three or four hundred, to judge by the noise they made crashing through the bush. We lay still, panting. It was too late to go any further. The natives were running along through the jungle, shouting to each other. I flopped over on my back. This way, I was relaxed and could keep from moving. Between the leaves of the small bush over my head I could see them coming. Some waved machetes, and three Japs in command carried heavy rifles.

"If anybody's caught," Krump whispered, "shoot. We'll all go down together."

The mob of natives rushed past with only a glance toward our hiding place—all but one. He stopped, peered at our clump of bushes, and walked toward us. He headed directly for me. I froze, terrified lest I make the slightest move to attract him. I held my breath, and tried not even to bat an eyelid. I watched his face for the first indication that he'd seen me. At the same time I listened intently to hear whether any of the other fellows made a sound. If so, it meant that they'd been seen, and we'd swing into action.

The native gave no sign that he saw us, but his next step forward was going to land right in my face. Drops of sweat rolled down my neck. Suddenly, a small bird in the tree above me attracted his attention. I squeezed my .45.

The Chamorro froze in his tracks, raised his machete, and struck out at a dead limb over my head. Then he turned and ran after the others. They took a downhill path and swept into the valley.

"My God!" cried Ski. "Is it worth it?" The strain had been terrific. It was the closest scrape any of us had had. We all laughed quietly in hysterical relief. As the sounds of the searchers breaking through the bush faded away, we climbed to our feet. We felt pretty good. It had been a tight spot, but we had pulled through. We clapped each other on the back, congratulating ourselves on being alive.

Ravenously hungry from the excitement and exertion, we ate our "lunch," the two slices of left-over coconut apiece. All that did was to whet our appetites.

Ski had charge of our small supply of water, and he rationed it severely. As we tilted our heads to drink, he watched our throats and jerked the jug down after the fourth swallow. Each man complained that he sweated more freely than the rest and so needed an extra swig, but Ski wasn't taken in.

When we'd rested, we cautiously pushed back to where we'd slept the night before to wait for the darkness to bring Manuel and food.

Night came, but no Manuel.

"Something's wrong," Krump decided. "I'll go take a look."

"For God's sake, bring back something to eat," Ski begged.

"Cool off, friend, I won't be gone long," replied Krump. Then he added, "I don't want to get lost. You men had better string out as guide posts along the way."

We set out together, a man dropping off at intervals of

a hundred yards or so—Johnston, then Jones, myself, Tyson, Ski—and Krump went on to the ranch.

In half an hour we heard Manuel's dogs bark, telling us Krump had arrived.

It seemed we waited ages there in the dark, fighting off the mosquitoes. I'd never been so hungry. All that any of us had eaten in the past twenty-four hours was the few slices of orange and coconut.

More than an hour later Krump returned, carrying a pail and a jug.

"What's the dope, Krump?"

"Anything the matter with Manuel?"

"What the hell have you been doing all this time?"

Everybody had a question.

"Sh-sh-sh-sh! Wait 'til we get back 'home,'" Krump shut us up.

"Okay, come and get it," he invited, once we'd reached our clearing. Each passed his coconut-shell cup, and Krump conscientiously divided equal portions of baked bananas and taro which had been diced and cooked in the milk squeezed from coconut meat. I'd never tasted anything so good. There wasn't half enough.

When we'd scraped the bottom, each passed his cup to Ski, who measured out a few spoonfuls of water. We washed our cups with this water, and then, since it was so precious and we were continually thirsty, drank it down.

"What about Manuel? How come he didn't show up?" Johnston asked as soon as we could think of something besides our hunger.

"Men, I've got bad news for you," Krump told us seriously.

We waited, absolutely quiet.

"The Japs have got Manuel."

"No!"

"My God! How'd it happen?"

"Jones, remember that piece of khaki you were going to patch your shirt with?" Krump asked.

"Sure, what's that got to do with it?"

"Well, you left it behind and the leader of the search party turned it in to the Japs. Since it was on Manuel's property, they arrested him and his brother Vicente, too."

"Jesus, that's the stupidest thing I ever did!" Jones sounded as if he were going to cry.

"It can't be helped now, Jones. Hell, if you hadn't slipped up, some of the rest of us would," Ski comforted.

"All I hope is Manuel don't get mad and kill one of those Jap bastards and get his head cut off," Johnston commented.

"Manuel's sister is plenty scared. She expects the Japs back any time. She cooked this food for us, but it's the last," said Krump. Then he added, "We can't stay here, anyway."

The Japs were drawing the net tighter. They had hunted us out of Juan Cruz's place. They had come within a foot of uncovering us this morning. Now they were breathing down our necks again. "We've got to get out of this territory," Krump continued, "and we might as well face it."

We decided to separate. We felt that the six of us couldn't travel together. We couldn't go fast enough, and we'd be bound to leave a trail. Going our separate ways suited me. I'd had enough experience in the outdoors so that I was inclined to trust my own decisions. But I didn't want to leave Al, and so I asked him to go with me. He agreed.

While we waited for "Jones's moon," which he said should be up any time now, the others began worrying about our knowing their secret hiding place and who was helping them. They trusted us, of course, but were afraid if the Japs caught us they might wring something out by torture. They're good at that.

Al and I talked it over quietly; then I said, "If the Japs catch either one of us, we swear that we will let them cut out our tongues before we will even so much as mention your names or say a word that can help them find you."

They looked at each other and nodded. "We swear the same," Krump answered for the four. We shook hands all around and sealed the oath.

Heavy hearted at leaving the only Americans we could hope to see for a long time to come, Al and I set out toward Manuel's place to pick up the homeward trail. As we drew near the house, we walked quietly to avoid rousing the dogs. Just as we got opposite the porch, however, they started yelping. Manuel's sister looked out the window, saw two khaki figures passing by, and withdrew from the opening. It was best to know as little as possible about men the Japs were hunting.

We had difficulty locating the main trail in the dark, but I found a small side path going in the right direction and it led us to the Ylig River. The water was waist high, and it was hard to find a place to cross. We took off our shoes and trousers and tied our shirt tails as high around our bodies as possible. I half-slid down the bank at a likely looking spot, but found it too deep to go more than a few steps. We didn't dare try to swim across with those heavy bags. I had climbed part of the way back up when we saw a light on the trail across the river. There, perhaps 150 yards away, was a Chamorro riding down the main path on a caribao, the buffalolike animals used in the fields. The native was holding above his head a flaming torch as he rode down the jungle trail.

"He may be searching for us," I whispered to Al. We plunged into the dark water, bags or no bags, and were across in a few minutes.

Dripping wet, we silently dressed. Another ordeal was in store for us. We still had to cross the treacherous swamp. Savagely pulling my shoe laces as tight as I could, I led the way, trying to pick out clumps of oozy grass to use as stepping stones. When I came out, nearly exhausted, on the other side, I sank down by a coconut tree. I thought Al was right behind me, but several minutes passed and he didn't show up. I strained my ears but heard nothing. Then I whistled, first softly, then louder, our prearranged call, meaning, "Come this way." From a great distance Al answered with our distress signal. I headed back and found him halfway across the swamp, standing helplessly on one foot.

"I've lost my shoe," he whispered. "This damn slush sucked it right off."

"God, that's bad. You'll have a hard time getting through the jungle without it."

For half an hour we plunged our arms up to the elbows into the mud, but it was hopeless. We gave up, leaving the shoe buried in the marsh.

At the coconut tree we sat down to rest. We'd been there, talking in whispers, for about five minutes, when I suddenly heard a rustle in the tall grass at my left.

"Al, there's somebody in those weeds," I whispered.

We'd been in the bushes about two months, and I'd learned to identify night sounds—a toad hopping through the dry leaves, a night bird lighting in a *kaful* tree, or a rat scurrying across the ground. I was sure I'd heard a man.

"Naw, you just imagine it," Al answered.

Then I heard another noise to our right, just a few feet away. Someone had forced his way through the bushes. It was very dark, "Jones's moon" having failed to make its appearance.

"There's somebody else over here," I whispered, pointing right, forgetting that I couldn't be seen in the darkness.

"That's just a toad," Al argued.

"A toad doesn't scrape through the bushes, Al."

I heard another rustling in the weeds at our left, several feet from where the first noise had come. Then another, almost in front, but slightly to our right. As a climax which made my heart drop to the bottom of my stomach, I heard someone stumble over a rock on the trail behind us. Our last avenue of escape was cut off.

"They've got us surrounded," I whispered.

Escape seemed impossible. We'd have to think fast. The man we'd seen on the caribao had come down the hill back of Manuel's ranch and had ridden down the trail either to get help or to notify the Japs. They'd had plenty of time to return while we were crossing the river and the swamp. They'd probably watched us as we used the flashlight while digging around in the mud hunting for Al's shoe. They'd seen us stop under the coconut tree and, as we sat there, had circled around us and were now closing in.

If these men were all Chamorros, I didn't believe they'd try to capture us. They wouldn't have guns, since the Japs didn't trust them with firearms. Neither of us had a gun, but I still carried the machete Francisco had given me. I didn't want to hurt any natives, but I was determined that, rather than be taken prisoner, I'd cut some of them down.

On the other hand, if they were Japs they'd be armed. They'd shoot us if we gave them the slightest excuse. Our only chance of remaining alive was to surrender.

I'd heard how the Japs had snatched wrist watches and other personal articles from Americans taken prisoner when the war first started. Some of the lousy little yellow rats who'd never owned anything in their lives had strutted around with an American watch on both wrists. I was determined that no Jap would ever wear mine if I could prevent it. I took it off and slipped it down inside my ankle-high shoe.

Then I remembered some notes I'd been keeping—a sort of diary—in which the names of the other Americans were mentioned. I didn't want it to fall into Jap hands. I took it out of my pocket and slipped it under a mass of tangled vines that encircled the coconut tree. I thought of the seven dollars sewn in the collar of my shirt and hoped they wouldn't find it.

All this took only a few seconds. Then I said, "Al, I think our only chance is to surrender. I may have been leader while we traveled through the bushes, but now our necks are at stake. I won't tell you what to do with yours. I'm going to offer to give up. You can stay here with me or take your bag and try to get away. If you want to run for it, I'll sit here quietly until you've had time to get in the clear."

"I don't want to quit now. I'm going up that hill above the trail. You come with me," Al replied.

"No, Al, I'm going to offer to surrender. I think that's

the best thing to do. Whatever you decide, act fast. Every second counts."

"I'm not going by myself," Al said.

I was glad to hear it. I didn't want to see him try to get away and be killed.

I called out, "We surrender! Come and get us! We have no guns!"

One man in the bushes on our right stood up and started toward us. We could see him silhouetted against the sky. He was only about twenty feet away. When he'd taken two or three steps, another man a few feet from him sprang up and with a loud, "Ssssssssstt!" grabbed him and pulled him down among the bushes out of sight.

I felt better. I knew they were Chamorros. We sat there another minute, but all was quiet. It was our move.

"Well, Al, it looks like they don't want us. We'd better get going." I spoke loud enough for the men in the bushes to hear.

We stood up, threw our bags over our shoulders and climbed the hill away from the swamp. As we crossed the trail where I knew at least two men had been stationed, I strained my eyes but could see no one. They'd hastily concealed themselves in the bushes bordering the trail. We pushed on up the steep hill beyond.

The going wasn't so good. My watch worked down to the bottom of my shoe and hurt my foot at every step. I stopped under a papaya tree, took off the shoe, and shook out the watch. It was still ticking, even though it was plastered with mud. I'd started tightening my laces when I heard two men coming up the hill toward us. I feverishly tied the knot and hurried on. In my excitement I forgot my watch and left it lying there on the ground.

We left the trail and started through the brush up the rough hillside. It was like a night compass run—without the compass—over ground carpeted with creeping *gado* roots spiked with long thorns. It was impossible to avoid stepping on them in the dark. Tyson, with only a sock protecting one foot, was really suffering. We had to make frequent stops. Finally we sat down, and I hurriedly made him a substitute for a shoe. I cut a bunch of twigs about half an inch in diameter and a little longer than his foot. With an extra pair of shoelaces, I tied the twigs together in a flat weave. Al held this against the sole of his foot while I wrapped and tied it with a strip of denim from some trousers I had in my bag. It was a cumbersome job, and he had trouble getting through the bush with that bulky wrapping slowing up every step. The twig platform hurt his foot, the long thorns still penetrated his flesh, but he hobbled on. The denim unwound itself continually and we were forced to stop again and again to "rebandage."

I led the way, holding the flashlight near the ground so we could both see. Struggling up the steep hillside, we cursed the *lemonchina* tearing at our clothes and skin and the *gado* thorns that penetrated leather soles as if they were cellophane. Our bags weighed us down. We salvaged six cans of food and the water jug and tossed the rest of our gear into the bush—extra clothing, everything.

By the time we reached the summit, we were so exhausted that, pursuers or not, we flopped down under a coconut tree and were dead to the world almost by the time we hit the ground. Two hours later we woke up, chilled by the night air.

Before starting out again, to lighten my load, I took my flashlight out of my shirt. The bulb had burned out, and since Al's battery had gone dead I was using mine in his case. I took the thick lens out of my flashlight and put it in my pocket.

As we went on along the top of the hill, we heard one native still stalking us. Sometimes he crept parallel to us, only a few feet of bush separating the hunter from the hunted.

"This guy can travel faster than we can. It's useless to try to outdistance him any longer," Al said.

"Okay. Let's stop awhile."

As dawn broke, we picked out a hiding place. The *gados* were thick and sported such healthy thorns that I had to take a stick and whack them off so that we could crawl through. Not five minutes later we heard our follower leave.

"He's gone to report to the Japs. He thinks we've bedded down here for the day. The search party will head straight for us," I told Al.

We were off in nothing flat. A hundred feet from the bottom of the hill we dived into a clump of bushes right near a native ranch house.

Half an hour later the search party came after us—two or three hundred of them. The Chamorros shouted to each other as they ran around peering into bushes. The Japs tried to shut them up, but they couldn't. We heard them near the spot we had just left, yelling, "Whooo-ooo! Whooo-ooo!" like farmers calling hogs.

We lay there all morning as the search party shuttled back and forth across the hilltop. We were completely defenseless.

That afternoon they swarmed down the hillside toward the spot where we hugged the ground. Not fifty feet behind us a small ravine cut into the hillside. One group after another jogged down the hill, stopped, and came over to investigate the stream bed. They walked back and forth, peering into the straggling bushes below, while we sat, almost too scared to breathe, for fear that one of them would come over in our direction. About an hour before dark the Japs called off the pack and sent them home.

Limp with fright and hunger we crawled out of our hideout and started up the hill, hoping to find some coconuts to slake our thirst. We wandered around in circles until by the stars we judged it to be three or four in the morning. We were tired and hungry and discouraged. We'd have surrendered if any Japs had been around to take us in.

Just when we felt worst, we came to a little one-room ranch house. We didn't even try to avoid it, but walked right up to the door. When we called, an old Chamorro let us in. His wife sat up on the mat on which they had been sleeping, native style, with their clothes on. They couldn't speak English very well but understood when we asked for something to eat. Just as the woman got up to go to the stove, we heard someone creeping up to the door. Al and I were ready to bolt when out of the night stepped a young man—completely naked!

"This is my son," said the old Chamorro.

The young man slowly began putting on his shirt and trousers.

"What were you doing out there without any clothes on?" I asked.

"I heard there were two Americans in the bush," he answered. "I took off my clothes so that no one could see me in the dark."

As he buttoned up his shirt he asked, "Don't you know me, Mr. Tweed?"

"I believe I've seen you somewhere before, I can't remember exactly where."

"I'm Manuel Aguon's brother, Vicente. I ran up ahead of the searching party on the hill to warn you they were coming."

"I'm sure glad to see you. Krump told us you and Manuel were in jail."

"We are. They beat Manuel every day. They keep asking, 'Where are the Americans?' but Manuel never answers. They don't know I helped you. I'm in jail because somebody told them I had a shotgun. They let me come home at night, but I have to report back every morning at five o'clock."

We told him how sorry we were about Manuel.

"I think they'll let him go soon. They see he won't tell," Vicente said proudly. Then he asked, "What are you going to do?"

We told him we were disgusted and on the point of surrendering.

"My friends, it's better that you don't think of that," he warned earnestly.

"We're fagged out. We've got to sit down and rest awhile, even if it's in a prison camp!"

"You're too late. You're not going to be put in any camp. They'll kill you."

Al and I were silent as Vicente went on.

"I talked by paper and pencil to a Jap Army officer. Eight years ago the University of Tokyo taught him to speak and write English. He doesn't remember how to pronounce words, but he can still write them. He told me that the Americans who surrendered when Guam was first captured had been taken away to Japan. I asked him, 'What about the others?' and he put down, 'Any American captured in the bush will be killed.' I wrote, 'If they come in and give themselves up, won't they be taken to Japan as prisoners?' He didn't answer. He just made a black line under the words that said 'will be killed.'"

That was the turning point in our flight. Now we had no choice. We had to stick it out or be executed. I made up my mind right then that the Japs would never take me alive.

6

EFORE the sun came up, we set out again, a little more
hopeful. Vicente had filled our water jug and told us
to go and hide and wait for him near the Pago Bridge
where there were plenty of thick bushes.

"I want to help you," he told us, "but I can't as long as I'm
a prisoner. I hope that in two or three days they'll set me
free."

Again I marveled at the loyalty of these natives. Here
Vicente was already under suspicion, his own brother being
flogged daily for befriending us, yet he dared to assist us
and wanted to do much more.

Vicente assured us it was safe to walk along the main road
until daylight. The Jap army had cleared out, he said, and
regular sentries had been removed from the highway. This
news pepped us up. We had been more discouraged by
having to struggle through the *lemonchina* than by anything
else. It was fine for temporary refuge, but hell for twenty-
four-hour traveling.

As we went down the trail, Al felt a lot better. Vicente
had given him one of a pair of rubbers to wear in place of
the clumsy wrappings around his foot. The overshoe, tied

on with a shoelace, was big and flopped around noisily at each step, but Al was as grateful as if it had been made to order.

When we struck the concrete road, we took off our shoes so that we wouldn't make any noise and headed for Pago. It was a long hike, but our lives were at stake. We'd gone about half a mile when we began to suspect that we were headed the wrong way. We were supposed to be going in the general direction of Agaña, which would put the hills on our left, the ocean on our right. After traveling half a mile, we could hear the waves plainly on our left, and turned around. We crossed the Ylig River bridge, climbed to the top of the hill on the other side and were just ready to start down when we heard the "Whooo-ooo! Whooo-ooo!" of the natives shouting at each other near the foot of the hill a quarter of a mile below.

"The bastards have a party down there watching for us," I swore in disgust. We couldn't afford to take chances. It had been bad enough when we were afraid of being taken prisoner. Now we knew we had a heluva lot more to lose. The important thing was to lay low and be quiet. We ducked off the road, and about fifty feet in, we happened on a well-concealed gravel pit where the natives had been digging out *cascajo* to pave the roads. We burrowed into a niche in the bank just big enough for the two of us.

All day we sat there without moving. We got terribly hungry but were afraid to cut into our small supply of tinned food, since we had only six cans left and didn't know when we'd get any more.

About three o'clock Al said, "We've got to eat *something*. I'll go nuts sitting here with nothing to do except think about how close we are to being six feet underground!"

After agreeing to a one-can quota, we deliberated like a couple of kids in front of a penny-candy counter before we could make up our minds which to open. I finally decided on corned beef. I could practically smell it just by looking at the beautiful helping pictured on the yellow label. Al chose pork and beans. " 'Pure, wholesome, nutritious,' " he read out, " 'serves three to four average portions.' I'll just make a liar out of that ad man. This is one can that won't be split four ways." And he devoured every bean and every spoonful of juice without stopping.

I thought I'd get along better if I ate only half of my corned beef at first, so I saved part of it for later.

"That meat'll spoil, sitting in that open can all day in this hot weather," Al warned.

I was afraid he was right that evening when I started to eat my second installment of corned beef. It was green around the edges. After smelling of it, I was inclined to throw it away, but thought, "Food's scarce, and I'm too hungry, anyway!" So I dove in. The strong tang puckered my mouth as if I were eating green persimmons.

"You'll get ptomaine poisoning," said Al cheerfully.

"What the hell! I couldn't be much worse off," I said and pushed the thought of the tainted meat out of my mind and suffered no ill effects.

After twelve hours, just as it was beginning to get dark and we were stretching our cramped legs to leave, we heard two men coming along the road. We sank down again. The men stopped right in front of the pit and talked for a few minutes. We couldn't hear well enough to tell whether they spoke in Japanese. Everything quieted down again as we heard one walk away.

"Al, I think those guys are lookouts. The Japs have stationed one right here and sent another on up the road. They know we're hiding somewhere in this vicinity and they expect to grab us when we come out tonight."

We were sure this was right when we heard the man sitting practically on top of us challenge a Chamorro who rattled by in a wooden-wheeled bull cart. It was a terrible disappointment to us. It meant we were stuck for the night.

We sat there in the dirt with our backs together for warmth. Our muscles ached, but we didn't dare stand up to stretch, even for a second. Cigarette smoke drifting to us from time to time told us the sentry kept his post. We could hardly stand to smell the smoke. It drove us crazy for a drag.

When daylight finally arrived, I warily raised my head above the pit. The guard was gone. To our right, where some old tires and rubbish were dumped, I made out a tiny trail. I investigated and found a native house barring our way. I retraced my steps.

"To get out, we'll have to cross either the road or the open field in front of a ranch house," I informed Al. "Now that we know how the land lies, maybe we can leave tonight."

With that hope, we were able to face another dreary, anxious day. Our one meal we varied by sharing pork and beans and corned beef. "May also be baked in a buttered casserole," Al read, torturing himself, as he ate the cold beans. This time we both ate our portions immediately.

We spent all day just sitting and hoping that the sentry would not be back again that night. "They'll think we've left this neighborhood by now," we told ourselves optimistically. But as the sun went down, we heard a car drive up and stop. The lookout was back! We were in for another night with our backs together against the cold earth.

The mental agony was almost unbearable. The cramps in our legs caused terrific pain. To add to our worries, I was afraid our joints might get so stiff we couldn't even walk, and I knew we'd need to be able to travel fast.

Near daybreak I said, "It looks like they're going to keep a guard here forever. Our only hope is to sneak out while he's off duty."

Al was so sore he said he knew he couldn't make it all the way to Pago.

"Vicente may not get out as soon as he thinks," he said. "I've been thinking about it. I'm going to Juan Mendiola's ranch. I know damn well he'll help me. You come, too."

"No, Al, we'd have to travel on the road for eleven miles to get there. That's taking too big a chance."

"Well, Juan's my friend, and I'm going."

I knew that I'd be better able to stay clear of the searching parties if I were alone, but since we'd started out together and Al couldn't find his way around in the bushes as I could, I was afraid he'd be caught. I didn't want him to go.

"Al, I've got a feeling I'm going to get out of this, and if you'll stick with me, we'll both come through. Why don't you stay?"

"No," he said. "I can't stand this being chased around any longer. I'm going to ask Juan to put me up."

There was nothing to do but let him go.

"What'll we do about the water jug?" he asked.

This was getting down to fundamentals. Possession of our one water jug might mean the difference between life and death.

"Let's match for it," I said.

We flipped coins, and Al won.

Then Al said, "I'll match my flashlight case against your battery."

We flipped again and this time I was lucky.

It was late in the morning when we painfully emerged from the pit. Crawling on hands and knees, we made our way to the highway. No one was in sight. Everything seemed quiet, so we stood up, crossed the road, and thankfully melted into the bushes on the other side.

"Okay, Ray, I'll be going."

"Good luck, Al."

"Same to you. Keep your fingers crossed."

We shook hands and parted.

I hated to see Al go. I felt very lonely. Now I'd have nobody to talk to, no companionship. I crouched in the *lemonchina,* not knowing where to go or what to do. Al was right. There was no guarantee when Vicente would be free. I wanted to go back to Juan Cruz's place, but I was afraid the Japs would be watching it.

Instead of traveling parallel to the road, I cut directly toward the ocean over jagged lava rocks concealed by dense shrubs. My downward trail brought me to a coconut grove near the sea. I looked around, afraid of finding a house or a path, but saw none. Nowhere was the grass broken from anyone's walking through it. I breathed more easily. With my machete I cut the noses off two coconuts and thirstily drank the milk.

My mind was crowded with problems. Chief among them was my lack of water and my lack of a jug in which to carry it even if I found any. The coconut grove was a godsend, but I couldn't stay here long. Sooner or later I was going to have to approach someone in order to obtain water. I considered going to a ranch house and asking for a supply. But how could I know whose house I'd run into? It might even be a Jap's or one belonging to a Jap sympathizer. I made up my mind that the best I could do would be to go back to see whether Juan Cruz could take me in.

As soon as I had reached a decision, I felt better. Down there near the blue sea in the sunny palm grove, everything seemed so peaceful. I could tell that many of the dark coconuts fallen off the trees had lain there for several years. There were no signs that any natives ever came to the spot. They usually leave the ground strewn with machete-slashed husks when they've dug out the white coconut meat. No such traces appeared anywhere in the grove. It was as if no human being had approached it for years. My dread of being caught dropped away from me. Under the influence of the quiet grove, my courage returned, and I thought, "It'll be better to go to Juan's now than to wait 'til dark. The Japs won't expect anybody to dare to travel in the daytime. If I can just stay out of sight, I'll be safer than at night."

I worked my way back toward the Ylig River bridge, sneaking up to the highway as I neared the structure. I looked up and down the road. It was deserted—no one in sight in either direction. Crossing the bridge was my greatest hazard. It was the only spot where I'd have to walk in full view along the open road. Suddenly, as I put my hand on the rail to cross, I saw a Ford truck parked at the other end, just off the concrete. In the quick glance I took, I saw a piece of cardboard with Japanese characters on it pasted on the windshield.

I ducked back into the shrubbery at my end of the bridge

and maneuvered into a spot from which I could see the car without being discovered. It was empty; no one was near; everything was perfectly quiet. I watched for half an hour before I could make up my mind to risk crossing the bridge. As I walked gingerly over it, I looked down to where the river emptied into the ocean and saw two Japs standing there fishing. My heart pounded for fear their poles wouldn't hold their attention until I was safely across. I made it!

On the other side, I struck out for the trail I knew would take me to Juan's. On the way I came upon a good-luck omen, a fresh-water spring. No one who hasn't been driven nearly crazy by thirst on a dusty island can know how good the sparkling water tasted. I drank and drank, washed my face, and drank some more.

I wasn't far from Juan's. I took no chances and kept to the bush. When I reached the edge of his property, I hid between tall stalks in his cornfield to wait for darkness.

Shortly after nightfall I heard someone coming down the path. I kept out of sight until, as the figure drew nearer, I recognized Sus Quitugua.

"Hey, Sus!" I whispered.

"Tweed!" he exclaimed. "Thank God you're safe. We've worried about you. Where've you been? Where's Tyson?"

I answered his questions, then got in a few of my own.

"Have the Japs bothered you and Juan?" I asked anxiously.

"No, everything's okay. We had one close call, though. The morning after you left here, the searching party came up with Ramón Baza leading, just like he said they would. They found two white insulators."

I cursed the haste which had caused me to leave behind two antenna transposition blocks. Juan hadn't had a

chance to come out to the shelter at daylight for a last minute check. A native had spotted the white blocks, shown
them to the others, and taken them to Baza.

Sus went on. "Baza called everybody together and said,
'These things were found here, but we're not going to turn
them in! Understand! We are going to forget all about it.
If I hear that any man mentioned this to the Japs, I'll kill
him!'" Not a word was ever said about the discovery.

Sus told me that our former shelter had been torn apart
and the canvas taken down.

"Try to make out in the bush tonight. Tomorrow, Juan
and I will find you a good place to stay," he promised.
Then, as if the thought had just occurred to him, he exclaimed, "Boy, I'll bet you're plenty hungry! I'll fix that.
You wait here."

I hadn't the slightest intention of leaving. In a few minutes he returned with fried eggs, rice, and a cup of milk. It
was the first decent meal I'd eaten in more than a week.
Tearing into it, I felt as if I'd really come home.

As I ate, Sus told me that Chief Myers and Dorsey Walker,
an electrician's mate who had also been stationed at the
Communication Office, had been in hiding in the bushes near
the coast between Piti and Sumay. A Chamorro operating
a motor launch for the Japs had been feeding them. When
they'd heard that the American prisoners were going to be
taken away to Japan, they went in and surrendered. I was
glad they'd got away safely.

Sus then announced, "The Japs have increased the reward money!"

It was swell that he'd saved that bit of news until after I
was fortified with supper.

"How much is it now?"

"A hundred yen for any American; a thousand for you."

"Whew! Looks like I'm mighty popular!" That was a lot of money now that the yen was pegged at the value of a dollar.

"They've got a special handbill with your picture on it."

"Where'd they get my picture?"

"Out of the photo album in your house."

"Those yellow devils!"

"Never mind," comforted Sus. "Nobody wants their dirty money. They won't try for the reward."

"I hope you're right, Sus."

Sus left, and I started looking for a place to sleep. I couldn't find anything that would pass for shelter, and so finally threw myself down under a coconut tree near the edge of the canyon.

I had been sleeping only a short time when rain spattering in my face shocked me awake. My clothes were soaked. I was chilled to the marrow. To keep my blood circulating, I stomped back and forth, flinging my arms around until three o'clock in the morning. Finally I was so tired that I could lie down on the wet ground and fall asleep in spite of the downpour. In an hour I woke up again, the rain still pounding in my face.

At the crack of dawn, still cold and wet, I started hunting for a safe place to spend the day. I went as far as the edge of the canyon and came to a dead stop. Within a few feet of where I stood rooted to the ground in plain sight, a man appeared. I recognized him as a native I'd seen at Juan's, but I didn't want a single soul to know that I was in that territory. I tried not to move a muscle that might attract his attention. He didn't see me although he passed near enough for me to touch him.

With his machete he began cutting bamboo poles. I
watched his every stroke so that the moment he got far
enough away I could move. He cut one pole and dragged
it back up to level ground. I retreated a few steps, freezing
in my tracks when he turned to come back, I knew that if I
stirred an inch I'd catch his eye. He made trip after trip,
carrying the poles he cut down. Each time he turned away,
I edged back a few feet. At last I'd put enough distance
between us so that I could afford to drop to my knees and
hit for the shelter of the brush.

That night I slipped up to the cornfield and waited for
Sus again. This time Juan was with him.

"It's sure swell to see you!" Juan exclaimed. "Where'd
you sleep last night?"

"Under a coconut tree in the rain."

"Ah, that's no good," he said sympathetically.

Sus said, "You could get sick and die! Tonight you come
to my house. My wife, my kids, and I will go to sleep at
Juan's like we used to."

I didn't want to put them out, but Sus insisted, and I went.
I was so exhausted I could hardly keep awake to eat supper.
When I went to turn in, there was no bed, but that didn't
bother me. I slept on the floor, but boards under my back
were a luxury compared to the rocky ground where I'd lain
for the past week. The mat was a special treat after the
previous night's session in the rain. I felt as fresh at daylight as if I'd slept on a feather bed.

Juan came over early and took me to a *pajun* jungle. Ordinarily it would have been a good hiding place, but one of
Guam's rainy spells was on, and as I crouched under the
long bayonetlike leaves, the water streamed down my back.
Everything was so damp that three magazines Juan brought

me swelled up, their pages sticking together so I couldn't read them. My clothes were sopping wet. The moment the rain let up, I'd take off my shirt and trousers, wring them out, and put them on again. As soon as I got them on, the torrent would pour down again.

I got soaked this way practically every day until, coughing and sneezing from the worst cold I ever had, I was afraid I was going to get pneumonia. Finally after three weeks the rain stopped.

Now that the rain was over, I was eager to finish the work on the radio and bring in some news. I was starving for information. Having been a radioman most of my life, I'd been a constant listener and was eager to get back on the air to find out what was going on in the world. I'd expected to be out of this mess by now, and I wanted to know why it was taking so long. Once, while Tyson and I were still together, he made out a calendar for December and another for January, 1942. "Shall I make another for February?" he asked me. "No," I'd said. "If the Americans aren't back by February, I'll eat that dog-eared deck of cards." Of course, February had come and gone without the Americans. I wanted to find out what was holding things up.

"Juan," I said, "we've got to put that radio in commission."

"Okay. I'll dig it up."

When I saw the corroded set Juan brought in, I was afraid it was ruined. He wasn't kidding when he spoke of "digging it up." He had buried the Silvertone near a flowering mango, and the battery was green with corrosion. Anyway, I worked on the receiver and put in the tubes. Juan got an automobile battery from a neighbor for the filaments, and we strung up an aerial between two coconut trees and hooked her up. It took a long time to warm up, then it began to whine, crackle, and finally sing—it worked!

At first I could barely hear the stations, they came over so faintly. Finally I brought one in fairly clear and heard a girl's voice giving the news. She was describing a big sea battle, and it sounded bad for us. The United States had suffered a severe defeat, she said, an entire task force had been destroyed. I was feeling pretty low when she signed off, and a man's voice announced, "This is Rad-yo Tok-yo bringing you the news!"

What a relief! Naturally I had more sense than to be taken in by a broadcast direct from Japan. I knew how reliable such "news" would be.

Although Tokyo Rose reported that the Jap fleet had knocked out the United States Navy, I wasn't discouraged. I knew she was lying about the results, but thought she might at least be right in saying there had been a fight. I felt certain that the Japanese had taken a beating, and it was good to know there was some action.

I was able to bring in stations in Japan, the Philippines, and China, but none from the States. Before the war, KGEI had been my favorite for news, and so I kept trying to get it, but had no luck. Then one night I was cruising the lower end of the dial and hesitated at one point at just the moment the announcer said, "This is KGEI, San Francisco!" I let out a whoop and shouted, "There he is! There's HOME!"

Very faintly I heard the first news I'd had from the States since the war started, nearly three months before. The Japs had landed on Java, the announcer said, and their planes were raiding Australia. They were making gains in Burma, too. Then he told about an American submarine captain who had sneaked his ship right into the harbor at Yokohama, where his vessel had rested on the bottom at periscope depth for thirty days. The Japs were building an aircraft carrier there and by cautiously raising his periscope for an occasional observation, he saw the Jap aircraft carrier under construction in a shipyard and realized that it was nearing completion and would soon be launched. He waited. Two—three weeks went by, but still he waited. At the end of a month his supplies were almost exhausted, and his men were on short rations. He would have to give up, for he had barely enough supplies to return to his base. He would have to leave that night. Before dark he took one last look. At the shipyard a huge crowd had gathered, and many flags were flying. The launching ceremony was in progress. Soon the carrier slid down the ways into the harbor. As it settled into the water, the submarine commander fired four torpedoes at close range. Each one found its mark, causing four violent explosions. The new Jap ship settled rapidly until it rested on the bottom. That was a piece of news Tokyo Rose had failed to mention.

With my radio finally in operation, a stir went through the island. The grapevine announced from ranch to ranch that the American radioman had got in touch with the United States again. Every evening as soon as it got dark and we dared hook up the radio, two natives would climb a pair of sixty-foot coconut trees some distance apart and string up the antennas.

By the time the program started coming in, forty or fifty people from near-by ranches had swarmed in to hear the news.

They scattered about in small groups, sitting on the ground and on logs, listening intently as the reports came

in. Between newscasts, while the radio was shut off to save
power, they talked loudly, laughed, and sang songs. I was
worried lest strangers be attracted to the gathering.

Each family brought me a present—eggs, bananas, oranges, or cans of food that they had concealed from the
Japs. They were very kind to me. What could I do?

The problem was solved for me. Japan and a station in
the Philippines came in for about four days—long enough to
whet our appetites for news thoroughly—then the fifth evening I picked up the battery and it was so hot it almost
burned my hand. It didn't last another day. No more
news, no more visitors.

Juan was very depressed. He'd carefully wrapped the
set in canvas before burying it, thinking that would keep
the battery dry. He hadn't realized that it would absorb
moisture from the ground. That was the end of the Silvertone. If we were to get more news, we'd simply have to
find a new radio and start all over again from scratch.

The Japs had discontinued their searching parties for the
moment, and I became less cautious. I went out in the late
afternoon to cut wood which I used as a smudge to chase
out the mosquitoes. Then I started going over earlier to
Sus's house in order to eat my evening meal while it was
still light.

One evening I had been at Sus's only a few minutes when
Josefina, Sus's wife, came running madly down from Juan's
shouting, "Run for the bushes. My father's at Juan's ranch
and he's coming down here."

I didn't get excited, for I'd found that when one of a family knew where I was, the rest was generally informed. I
couldn't understand what all the excitement was about, but
I got up and started slowly toward my hideout.

"Hurry! He's a Jap!" shouted Fina.

That was all I waited to hear. I went so fast through those bushes back to my hideout that I almost made a new trail.

I remained hidden until Sus came and gave me the all-clear signal. I asked him, "What did Fina mean about her father being a Jap?"

"Sure," he answered, "didn't you know that my father-in-law is a Jap? His name is Yamaguchi. He's the big-shot Jap down in Asan. His wife is a Chamorro."

Each town or district had its "big-shot" Jap. Yamaguchi was, of course, a collaborator with the military forces, conferred with them and passed their instructions along to the district commissioner, who was generally a Chamorro. Things weren't as safe for me as I had thought they were.

At this time I learned that Sus had taken it upon himself to buy all my food, since Juan had a struggle to provide enough for his wife and thirteen children. Once Sus had run out of money to buy any more groceries at all—not even rice. He didn't breathe a word to me about it. He sold his bicycle, his only transportation other than by foot, for fifty yen and spent it on food for his family and me. When that was gone, he got down his .20-gauge shotgun from the top of a breadfruit tree where he'd hidden it from the Japs, found a buyer for it, and kept the supplies coming in. I was eating every day without fail, but there were undoubtedly times when Sus went hungry. I told Juan I'd have to leave.

Next day Juan announced, "Got a swell place for you. My brother Manuel says he'll let you stay in a cave on his ranch. It's nice and dry."

"A cave! Wonderful." I'd been rained on and chilled through so many times in the past that the prospect of a dry earthen floor and possibly some nice hard boards to sleep on raised my spirits as much as if I'd been promised the admiral's cabin.

Juan's brother, Manuel, came for me in the morning. I had heard of Manuel Cruz—he was well-known in his district. Rather small, he carried himself with an air of self-importance.

"Okay, come," he said somewhat officiously, I thought. "Come, you stay chicken house first." He spoke very little English.

He led me to a ramshackle old house which had been converted into a glorified chicken coop. I noticed, however, that he stored his corn there, and so I knew the place would be dry. I thanked him and he left.

He returned almost immediately with a pleasant stout native woman and a young man of about twenty-five.

"Wife," he grunted.

We nodded to each other.

"Pedro Cruz."

We shook hands.

"Your son?" I asked.

"No relation," Pedro spoke up.

I knew there were many persons on Guam with the same name who don't claim kinship. First cousin is as far as they count.

After only one night in the chicken house, Manuel walked in and announced, "Move!"

"Swell. We go to the cave now, eh?" I asked in anticipation.

"No. Cow pasture."

He led the way to a large field in one corner of which stood a small tin-roofed shelter. He brought me a wicker chair that had a rack underneath which pulled out to make a foot rest.

"Thanks, Manuel, I can sleep in this."

"You like oranges?" he asked abruptly.

"Sure."

He disappeared and in a few minutes returned with a couple.

I stayed in the cow pasture two days. On the third morning Manuel came by and informed me, "We go work in fields at Maleyok. Be gone all day. Nobody bring you food."

"Forget it. I won't starve," I reassured him, and he left.

As noon came, and I began to get hungry, I thought of the oranges Manuel had brought me the day before. "The tree must be right around here," I thought. "It didn't take him two minutes to get them. I'll take a look."

Sure enough, I found the tree, picked two oranges, and was about to peel one of them when suddenly Manuel appeared.

"So, you steal my oranges!" he accused in an angry voice.

At first I thought he must be joking, then I saw he meant it.

"I didn't consider it stealing, Manuel. I'm not a thief. If you feel that way about it, take the oranges."

"Oh, no! You steal them. You keep them," he snorted, and strode away.

I didn't know what to make of it. "What kind of a man is this?" I asked myself. Was I doing the right thing to put myself in his hands? Why should he act like this? What would he do next?

The next thing he did was perfect. He took me to the cave.

7

IT WAS all I had hoped it would be. Technically speaking, it wasn't really a cave, but a shelter formed by an enormous rock which lay on the side of a hill overlooking the sea. It was perched on other rocks so that there were open spaces beneath it. One space made a room of two different floor levels. The first consisted of a fairly level spot of ground which was just large enough to make a good place for me to sleep. About fifteen feet away and eight feet higher, the slanting, rocky floor of the second level was covered with dirt which had spilled down into the cave. I built a two-foot retaining wall below this, filled in with stones, and then smoothed it all over with loose dirt and decomposed rock to make the upper floor. I had no shovel for this work, but used only my machete and bare hands. I made a floor of four eight-inch boards, and when I'd finished I had an upper story where I kept my wicker chair and two boxes that held my canned goods.

There were two ways of getting into the hideout. One was to climb up the hill and enter from below. The other, which I used, was to enter from above, going down a ver-

tical ten-foot cliff, in which I chiseled notches large enough
to make steps.

Sus Mesa, a well-to-do farmer of the district, brought me
a pair of binoculars that had belonged to the former Beach-
master's Office. By climbing up on top of the large rock,
I had a good view of the ocean, though practically none
of the coastline. The mouth of the Ylig River was in full
sight, and across it I could distinctly see an enormous cave
in which a Chamorro family boiled down saltwater in a
huge iron kettle to make salt. I spent hours watching them
through my binoculars as they carried water for their kettle,
carried wood for the fire, and kept the fire going. It helped
to pass the time.

Thanks to my friends of the Yoña District, I began to
enjoy comfort again for the first time since the December
blitz. It was now March. Manuel's wife brought me a mat
to sleep on and a pillow stuffed with kapok, which grew all
over the island. Others appeared with canned goods, which
I accepted gratefully as fast as they brought them. Provisions stacked up on the upper level. For the first time
since I had taken to the bush I had more than I could eat.
For breakfast, I had a wide choice—orange juice, grapefruit
juice, or grapes.

I took up life in my new home with a good deal to be
thankful for. For the first time in over three months, I felt
that I had successfully eluded the Japs long enough to enjoy a breathing spell and get ready for the next chase. I
had a good chance to remain hidden indefinitely if people
wouldn't talk and give me away. My cave was well concealed, and I was already turning over in my mind the
ways in which I would make it more comfortable.

First, to me, comfort meant getting the news. Juan

brought over a friend, Joaquín Limtiaco, who had been a regular listener to the broadcasts at Juan's place. I'd known Limty in Agaña, where he operated a fleet of taxicabs. He was one of those good-natured, happy-go-lucky fellows who always know the right man at the right time.

"Limty, you've always got your ear glued to Guam's 'coconut grapevine'; you ought to be able to tell us how we can get a radio."

He beamed.

"Actually," I hastened to explain, "there's more to it than just the set. There's the radio itself and then the power to generate it."

"I don't know about the radio just now, but I know where I can get a gasoline-driven generator," Limty said enthusiastically. "It puts out 110 volts a.c., and it's portable. We can bring it down in a Ford truck."

"That's keen. I can get a car battery, set it up by the side, and use it to start the engine. Then I can charge the car battery on one voltage while the generator runs, and also plug it on 110 volts."

Limty brought the generator, and we set it up. Then he pulled a socket and a 100-watt electric-light bulb out of his pocket. He was way ahead of me. I hadn't thought of that. Naturally, if we could generate power for the radio, we could have lights. That bright bulb, in a country section where electricity hadn't reached even the best homes, brought the final touch of luxury to my cave.

We were all impatient for a radio now that the power was all set for it, but again we faced the difficult problem of finding one after the Japs had already gone over the island with a fine-toothed comb.

Then Juan, still fretting about his part in the tragedy of

the Silvertone, brought around Sus Mesa, who, like Limty, also had a wide circle of acquaintances.

"Oh, radio!" he repeated knowingly when I broached the subject. "You want to come with me?"

This was worth taking a risk for. We bounced in his jitney to the home of Jesús Crisostomo, whom, as it happened, I had known at the Communication Office, where he also had worked.

"You're welcome to my home," he said as we entered, and went on to apologize, "I'm sorry I don't have anything to offer you to eat. The Japs took everything. I've plenty of crops planted, though, and if you'll come again in two or three weeks. . . ."

"I don't need food, Jesús," I said. "I came to see if you can get me a radio."

"A radio!" He looked at me as if I had asked for a battleship, but I thought he had the same knowing tone in his voice that Mesa had used. I went home pretty bucked up.

Two nights later, in came the radio. Jesús and his brother had risked their lives to get it. In the dead of night they had jimmied a window of the schoolhouse—now used as a Jap storeroom—and stolen the set.

Again, as soon as I saw the radio, I recognized it as one that had been brought to me for repair. This one, a large Zenith, had belonged to Lieutenant Eppley, a Navy doctor. In fact, it had been in my shop when the Japs came. Its voltage divider had burned out. This advance information saved me a lot of time. Knowing exactly what was needed, I tore some resistors out of the useless Silvertone, and soldered them across the divider. After making a few more necessary adjustments, I plugged it in and started up the gasoline engine. When I turned on the radio, a loud roar

came from the speaker. The spark-plug noise was feeding
through the line to the radio. Only two or three powerful
stations could be heard above the din, and they were Jap
stations. I didn't want them.

After much finagling, I picked up a vibrator unit such as
is used with an auto radio. We were on the air again,
operating from a car battery.

The first station I picked up came in on 9640 kilocycles,
the Philippine frequency. The broadcast was in English
and came from an "underground" station on Corregidor.
Calling itself The Voice of Freedom, it described the heroic
stand being made by our men in the garrison there. I took
heart from the words. They made me realize that even
though I was in a tight spot, plenty of other Americans
were sweating it out in blood and not uttering a word of
complaint.

Since my cave was small, only a favored few could come
to the broadcasts, which was all right with me. Eight or
ten of us sat on the lower level as near as we could crowd
to the radio placed atop two boxes on the upper level. My
most interested listener was Manuel, who regularly as clock-
work every evening brought down his wife and four children for the program from KGEI. With his poor English,
he had a hard time understanding the announcer, so that
although he put his ear close to the loud-speaker and listened attentively until the last word of every broadcast,
when it was over he'd invariably look up at me and ask,
"What's the news?"

Since Manuel was good enough to let me stay on his property, at considerable risk to himself, the least I could do was
to see that he got a full account of what was going on. I
took full notes of every broadcast and gave them to his

wife, who read and spoke English. She relayed the information to him in Chamorro.

It was this making out a nightly report that gave me the idea of starting an underground newspaper. From Paul Muña, a native who had worked at the Commandant's office, I obtained an old but usable typewriter and some paper and carbon, and the *Guam Eagle* was born. I took the name from the mimeographed daily formerly run off at the Communication Office before the Japs came.

Each night I typed up my notes into front-page news. At first I made only two copies, an original for the "files," and a carbon for Manuel. He was as proud of it as a squirrel is of his tail, and always took his sheet home with him. He couldn't read it, but he listened importantly, nodding his head as his wife and Pete interpreted it to him. I cautioned them against telling anyone about the *Eagle* or showing it to outsiders, but it was not long before they, with typical native inability to keep a secret, were taking it all over the neighborhood and letting people see it and even make duplications of it. Once Sus Mesa's niece copied it and showed it to all her neighbors. "I know this is straight news," she told them. "Tweed got it on the radio and this is exactly what he heard." I saw to it that she didn't come over again.

Others to whom I was indebted for food and clothing begged to be put on the *Eagle's* subscription list, until our "printing" establishment was turning out a mammoth daily edition of five copies. This was total capacity, since the typewriter simply couldn't produce a sixth legible sheet. No one seemed to think of asking me to run off a second "printing."

To put a stop to the paper being passed around until it

fell into Jap hands, I laid down certain rules that all subscribers pledged themselves to abide by. No one should
tell where the sheet came from. No item should be copied.
Each edition was to be destroyed by fire as soon as it had
been read.

Although the subscribers observed the rules, circulation
of the news itself soared by word of mouth. Hundreds of
persons received accounts of what was going on at least
once or twice a week. I didn't welcome the publicity, but
I accepted the responsibility, and through my paper carried
on morale operations against the Japs. I became a kind of
Office of War Information for Guam.

The four months during which I published the paper were
a difficult period in the history of the war. During this
time Corregidor and Bataan fell, but the *Eagle* never lied,
no matter how black the news. If we shot down only two
Jap planes and lost an aircraft carrier, that's what the paper
stated. I operated on the principle that truth is the best
propaganda. Naturally I knew that the news from KGEI
would be more accurate than that from Tokyo or Manila,
and so I based my reporting on the broadcasts from the San
Francisco station.

I was absolutely sure, of course, that America would come
out on top, and so I selected significant items of the news
which pointed in that direction and elaborated on them.
One incident concerned the activities of a single American
destroyer in enemy waters. The United States warship met
a fleet of Jap transports escorted by four Jap destroyers.
In the face of the concentrated fire of all the Jap guns, the
Americans charged and sank one destroyer, then wheeled
to escape. The three remaining gave immediate chase, but
fortunately a sudden tropical rainstorm hid the American

ship. Then, under cover of the heavy downpour, the United States warship circled back and sank two of the transports while the Jap destroyers were searching vainly in the rain.

I used this in an editorial as an example of the daring and imagination of our Navy. Americans didn't have to rely entirely on superior force of arms but could outwit and outfight their enemy even when we were at a disadvantage. In a short time this story was being repeated in all corners of Guam.

The best news we got in the whole time the radio was in operation was the announcement of the Doolittle raid on Tokyo on April 18, 1942. The Japs had been boasting that Japan was surrounded by an invincible ring of steel in the form of the Imperial Navy and Air Force. When Juan heard of the bombing, his eyes lit up, and he said, "Boy, I hope Doolittle comes by here on his next trip!"

Islanders' faith in the eventual return of the Americans remained high all through the occupation. There were a few who finally decided that the United States Navy was never going to return, that the Japs were there to stay, and that it would be best to collaborate with them. But they were a very small fraction of the population. If I had to guess, I'd say perhaps two hundred out of the twenty-four thousand. The others remained steadfast in their faith in the United States. The high degree of confidence had been built up through the years by what Americans had done for Guam, but my *Guam Eagle* had its tiny part to play, and I was proud of it.

8

M Y CAVE became a rendezvous. It was growing more comfortable all the time. My radio sat on two boxes and screened the car battery, to which I attached wire running to both "rooms." The wire provided current for 32-candlepower automobile-headlight bulbs which I'd secured to the ceilings. I took bright tin cans and made reflectors for the lights, using my 110-volt generator to heat the electric soldering iron to join the reflectors to the bulbs. My native friends enjoyed the light, much brighter than that cast by coconut-oil lights in the ordinary shack of the country sections.

In exchange for world news supplied by the radio and the *Guam Eagle*, I received a steady flow of supplies and local intelligence from a few trusted friends. One of these was Tommy Tanaka, a twenty-six-year-old half-Japanese and half-Chamorro. He was good looking, larger than the average native, smart and quick. He talked lickety-split in good English and no sooner received an idea than he carried it out. He was a devout Catholic and absolutely trustworthy. Tommy knew as well as I did that eventually the Americans were coming back. He had liked living in

Guam before the Japs came, and he hated it now. By risking his life to help me, he proved that he was loyal to the United States.

On every trip Tommy came laden with large quantities of canned food—vegetables, corned beef, and fruit. I'll always be grateful to him for a priceless package of razor blades, a pocket mirror, and a toothbrush and toothpaste. These valuable goods came from the grocery store where he worked. It belonged to Mrs. Dejima, a full-blooded Japanese woman who also was strongly pro-American. She scorned the *obi* and the kimono and always wore American clothes. Long after traffic in American money was a criminal offense, punishable by whipping, Mrs. Dejima continued to accept dollars when doing so would help a native.

Luisa Guzman told me how Mrs. Dejima had come into disfavor because of her sympathies. Luisa had worked as housekeeper for Mr. Walker, foreman of the plumbing shop in Agaña Navy Yard. When the Japs locked up the Americans as prisoners of war, the girls who'd worked for them took them clothes, food, and cigarettes.

Luisa wanted some cigarettes for Mr. Walker and turned to Shinahara for help. As she had taken care of his children when they were sick and done him other favors, she felt he would reciprocate her kindness.

"Mr. Shinahara, will you give me three cigarettes for Mr. Walker?" she asked.

"Hell, no!" said the traitor merchant. "Nothing for the Americans!"

Then she went to Mrs. Dejima, asked the same questions and came away with a full carton of Walker's favorite brand.

Mrs. Dejima gave other indications of her sympathy for Americans until on two different occasions she was taken to headquarters and flogged with a bull whip. Still she remained steadfast in her loyalty.

She wasn't supposed to know that her clerk was carrying provisions from her shelves to my cave, but I had an idea that she did. I thought she was smart enough to realize that it was best to have in mind as little such information as possible if the Japs started grilling her.

One day when Tommy came in with some cigarettes and canned food, he sat down to talk with Pedro Cruz and me.

"Many differences between Guam fruits and vegetables and United States ones, no?" observed Pedro.

"Your mangoes are delicious. They taste like a cross between our peach and apricot. Too bad we don't have them at home," I said.

"You have one 'strawberry,' I hear," said Tommy. "That must be good."

"It is, but we have spinach, too, so don't feel bad. You're lucky not to have that. Chinese cabbage is much better." Taro, bananas, pineapples, and guavas all received my high praise.

"There's one American fruit in the Navy commissary I like very much," Pedro said. "It's round. It's heavy. It's got a thin peeling."

"Do you mean an apple?"

"No."

"Plum?"

"No."

"Orange?"

"No."

I gave up.

"I don't know what you call it in English," he said, "but in Chamorro we call it 'potato.'"

People in the neighborhood came to *el Americano* on problems connected with the war and Jap occupation of Guam. José Torres, who lived on a ranch six miles down the road, was worried about whether to sell his house in town. The Japs, thinking that they were on Guam to stay, began buying some of the better homes. "Buying" is really a courtesy term, for the purchasers set their own prices, usually amounting to about one-sixth the fair value.

José said that when a friend of his who owned several houses in Agaña refused to sell, they put him in jail and tortured him until he changed his mind. After that, the natives felt it was useless to resist the "bargain" offers.

José had been offered only 2,000 yen for a house which had cost him $6,000 to build. Although the invaders had declared the yen equal to the dollar, José knew that before the Jap occupation it was worth only a quarter of that. It didn't take him long to figure out that they were trying to give him $500 for a $6,000 house.

What worried José was that in the "legal" transaction, he would have to give the Japs a bill of sale. "When the Americans come back, won't they confiscate all Jap property, including my house?" he asked.

"No. Americans don't recognize any agreement made under pressure," I assured him. "Any time you're forced to sell something or sign any paper under threat of torture, it's illegal. When the Americans return, you'll get your house back."

I didn't know the details of the law on real estate matters, but I knew American ways well enough to be certain that José would get fair play and that our government wouldn't keep his house.

He breathed a sigh of relief. Then he asked, "When the Americans come and give me back my house, will I have to pay them the 2,000 yen the Japs give me for it?"

This was a fine point. I studied a minute before coming up with an answer to that one. "No," I concluded, "because the money you'll get for your house now is Jap money. When the Americans return, it won't be worth a dried mango seed. Nobody'll accept it."

José left the cave that night an even firmer believer in America than he was when he entered.

Limtiaco was one of my most frequent visitors. One day he asked me if I'd like to have a gun. I said, "I certainly would." He told me that three American officers had "sat out" the first Jap attack in a ranch house near his own. When they left, they apparently intended to surrender, for they took off their guns and left them behind, not wanting to turn over such loot to the enemy. On Limty's next trip he brought me a pistol belt, a .45 completely loaded, and two spare clips of ammunition. This made twenty-one rounds—three clips with seven rounds in each one. It was a pretty old gun, but it had been well taken care of and wasn't rusty.

From that day, the .45 was my closest companion. It gave me a feeling of confidence. I felt that if I got in a tight spot, I might be able to shoot my way out. At night I laid it close by my side and got so I'd automatically reach over and grasp it whenever I woke in the darkness.

I polished it carefully, and although it was almost impossible to keep rust from accumulating on the outside of the barrel, I always kept the inside shiny and clean.

My most distinguished visitor at this time was Dr. Ramón Sablan, a forty-two-year-old, keen-faced Chamorro. He was Guam's only native doctor, and very popular. Before the war he'd done a lot to educate the people to keep the villages sanitary.

"How're you feeling?" he asked me.

He'd heard that there was a sick American in the bush, and he was risking his life to come and treat him. I was perfectly well, and so we had a social visit. As he left, he said, "Any time you need a doctor, just get word to me and I'll come out and take care of you."

I learned later that he went up to Manengon and stayed there three days treating Krump for a sprained knee.

Few women came to see me, and so I remember a young girl, Joaquina Okazaki, very well. In spite of the fact that she was half Japanese, both she and her Chamorro mother hated the Japs as much as we all did—and with good reason. Some years previously Joaquina's father had visited Saipan. While there he had too much to drink in a public bar and incautiously raised his voice in telling how much better off people were in Guam than in Saipan under the Japanese rule. Someone touched him on the shoulder, he was taken away, and his head was cut off.

His widow came to see me, bringing a note from her daughter asking if there was anything I needed; if so, she'd like to provide it. I told her I'd like something to read, and on the next trip out her mother brought me some magazines and books. In her next letter Joaquina wrote, "Ask my mother to let me come to see you." So I did.

And Joaquina came out. She was a nice looking girl, around twenty-six, I'd guess. She was about five feet tall and had a trim figure. She didn't show her Japanese blood.

I thanked her for the magazines and books, and we were quite friendly. As she was up on all the local gossip, I enjoyed her visit. Among the valuable things she told me were the names of several men who were trying to find me in order to collect the reward.

As she was leaving, she asked whether there was anything else I needed. Several men had tried to get two radio tubes, but without success. I'd see what she could do. I told her the types I needed.

A week later, Joaquina was back, a brown-paper package under her arm. She had a surprise for me. She unwrapped a hand-sewn dark-blue shirt—just what I needed for traveling at night. I gave her my sincere thanks. Then she handed me the two radio tubes I'd wanted. "The things a woman can accomplish!" I thought. I knew she must have gone to a lot of trouble to get them. When I told her how grateful I was, she said seriously, "I know the Japs can't win this war. I want to help you so when the United States Navy comes back to Guam you can tell them that I am a good American and they won't put me in jail for being half Japanese."

The most comforting call I had was from Tonie, a Chamorro girl of nineteen. I'd seen her often before the war at Chief Myers', where she worked as housegirl. She and her mother were now living with Juan Cruz's family, and she used to bring me fresh vegetables and melons. She was very worried about me and one day told me with childlike sincerity how I could escape from the Japs for good. She said that her uncle knew a man who was in contact with the *taotaomona* or "ancient people" of Guam. Most Chamorros will laugh and deny the stories about these little people of legend, but just the same few will deliberately go out of their way to anger them.

Tonie believed in them implicitly. Her uncle's friend had a *taotaomona* helper, she said, by whose aid he was able to carry heavier loads and swim farther than ordinary men. Her uncle noticed his friend would never enter a church, but always sat outside by the door and listened to the ritual from there—a sure sign he was in touch with the mythical people.

"You need the *taotaomona*," Tonie insisted. "They are very strong and can protect you. They can hide you so nobody will ever find you. They live in caves by the sea and are never seen by anyone, but my uncle can bring you together through his friend."

"What will I have to do to get them to help me?"

"Give up God and pray to the devil!" she answered, opening her eyes very wide in awe of her own words.

I thought the devil probably would have plenty of pull with the Japs, but, hard up as I was for such influential friends, I declined.

The Chamorros were growing to hate the Japs more all the time, Limty told me. Hardly a day went by but what several natives were tortured. The Japs had changed the traffic to the left-hand side of the road. Many local people, used to the American system of right-hand lanes which they'd used for years, forgot the new regulations. When this happened, the Japs took pleasure in slapping the driver.

One night Limty came in all excited.

"We're organizing," he said. "We're gonna throw the Japs out!"

The Japs, the natives estimated, had withdrawn all their fighting forces from the island except 150 sailors. Limty and his friends intended to lay their plans carefully and kill all 150 on the same night. They wanted me and the other Americans to help.

It was a swell idea. Nothing could have pleased me more than to wipe out the little beasts all at once. But I knew it wouldn't work. I said to Limty, "All right, you kill these Japs here. So what? You're absolutely defenseless. You can't hold off Jap planes. You can't keep Jap warships from landing troops. When they do and find the garrison wiped out, they'll kill every last person on Guam—men, women, and children!"

Limty was depressed. He'd been aching to shoot up some Japs.

"Wait 'til the Americans come," I said. "The minute they land, you can swing into action. Kill every Jap you can then. The return of the Americans is our only hope."

Although I had many callers, I missed the company of the other Americans who had gone to the bush. Juan told me that they were back at Manengon. I got in touch with them, and they made the trip down the hill and across the swamp to see me. They were in good spirits. Manuel Aguon was out of prison. The fellows swore by him. They spent their days in the bush and their nights in the loft of an old house on his property. They said the *Guam Eagle* was one of their few bright spots, and I promised I'd set aside a copy for them each day and they could pick up the back numbers whenever they came down.

One night Manuel brought Jones and Ski to visit me. Limty had just given me some liquor, and so I asked the boys if they'd like a drink of Canadian Club.

"Don't kid us, Ray," complained Ski, in a voice full of sad remembrance. "We've been in the bush too long to take that sort of joking."

"I'm not kidding," I laughed and broke out a fifth.

At first they thought it was some native drink behind a Canadian Club label. By the time they had thoroughly smelled it, tasted it, and were convinced, the bottle was empty.

Then they were so brokenhearted that the liquor was all gone that I brought out a second fifth. Jones and Ski were riding high by the time they were ready to go home. Jones had asked me to get him a toothbrush. I handed it to him, together with a tube of toothpaste, and they set out.

I heard later that when they crossed the Ylig River on the raft Manuel had made, Jones was so tipsy that his foot caught between the bamboo poles of the raft and he fell off in midstream, sweeping the others overboard with him. The water wasn't deep, and Ski and Manuel waded ashore. Jones, befuddled, began swimming upstream, getting nowhere fast.

"For crying out loud, Jones, stand up and walk across!" Ski yelled.

Jones put his feet down and found himself in water hardly up to his waist. After that, Ski took the greatest delight in kidding Jones about his swimming party in the Ylig River. "And to top it all, he lost his toothpaste!" he'd roar. He got more laughs out of that incident than from anything else that happened while we were in the bush.

Juan Duenas, whom I had known at the Navy Commissary where he worked before the war as a storekeeper first class, Navy Insular Force, had been coming from his near-by ranch to see me and read the news. One evening he handed me a note. It was from Mrs. Johnston, one of the island's most prominent citizens. She had been a schoolteacher and principal of the Washington School. Before the war, her husband, an American, had owned and operated the Gaiety Theater, one of Agaña's two movie houses.

"Please," wrote Mrs. Johnston, "will you put me on the list to receive the *Guam Eagle?* You know, my husband is now in Japan in a prison camp. I wouldn't worry so much if I could only read the news of how America is planning to rescue him and the others who are being held."

"Do you know Mrs. Johnston well?"

"Yes," John assured me. "She's a good woman, very careful."

I wrote an answer, telling her I would be glad to send her the paper and warning her to use discretion with regard to the news that was published. I signed the note *J. C.* These initials stood for the name which the natives gave me. They had decided I was to be called Joaquín Cruz if the time came when they had to refer to me in the presence of enemies.

Mrs. Johnston answered that she would be very discreet, and I began sending her the news sheets. She didn't get them regularly every day. Prompt delivery of the new *Eagle* wasn't its strongest selling point. As I typed each edition, I put the initial of the subscriber in the upper left-hand corner and set it aside in a neat stack to be called for in person or by a friend. One copy a day went to Limty, Tommy, the Americans at Manengon, Mrs. Johnston, and a neighbor, Felix Torres. Sometimes it was three or four days before the Americans at Manengon received their copies, but even so they were far better informed about the outside world than many people on Guam.

Some days after I'd been sending the *Eagle* to Mrs. Johnston, Juan came over to tell me that she'd invited me to her ranch house.

I hesitated to accept. I'd been venturing along the road at night to Juan Cruz's house half a mile away, but Mrs. Johnston's ranch was six miles toward town. A real get-together did appeal to me, though, and so when Limty reminded me that we'd heard nothing of Jap patrols for some time and added, "We won't walk—we'll go by jitney," I agreed.

We arrived about nine o'clock in the evening. At the door we were met by Mrs. Johnston, her son Herbert, her two daughters, Marian and Cynthia, and her son-in-law, Joe Torres. Before the war Joe had owned a bar in downtown Agaña. When the Japs came, he had managed to hide a few cases of good liquor on his ranch. Tonight he brought out some Walker's De Luxe—and *ice!* This was the first time I'd had a drink—any drink—with ice in it since Tyson and I had taken to the bush five months before. I certainly enjoyed that highball!

Actually, no appetizer was needed for the delicious feast Mrs. Johnston provided. We sat down to young barbecued pig, surrounded by steaming *taro*. A glass of milk and cookies fresh from the oven ended a meal that seemed too good to be true to a man whose main kitchen utensil for half a year had been a can opener. After dinner Marian passed around small glasses of *tuba*, the sweet liquid obtained from the bud of the coconut tree, a favorite drink of mine.

Conversation in ordinary times would have been light

and fast and loud. There would have been music and singing and amusing stories about local characters. That night
we laughed infrequently, and usually at rather grim subjects for humor.

John Flores had been in Agaña that day and had heard
that the Japs had German police dogs which they were
trying to put on my trail. He said that the townspeople
were laughing over a fight in which one of the big dogs had
been chewed up by a smaller native pooch. A Jap officer
had pulled his pistol and shot the native dog to save the
German police.

I asked whether the German police dogs were well trained
and what scouting methods the Japs were using with them.
From John's report it seemed that they weren't enjoying
any great degree of success.

"These dogs they have are no good," he told us. "They
are stupid. They can't be taught to pick up a trail."

I said, "In order to teach a dog to do anything, you have
to know more than the dog."

Everyone laughed uproariously—louder and longer than
the remark deserved, just because the excuse came so sel-
dom to any of us those days.

We all got a kick out of the way Cynthia described something that happened at the district school. It was a local
custom for the young people in the district to have a party
each Saturday night at the schoolhouse where they'd fur-
nish their own amusement—dancing, singing, and playing
the guitar, piano, and banjo. The Japs took over these
parties, and their own master of ceremonies tried to use
them for purposes of propaganda. "Everything that is any
good is made in Japan," he said. "The good songs come

from Japan; even this piano was made in Japan. Now, let's have some music."

Then he asked for someone to play. The Chamorros looked around for some of the Japs to volunteer, but none knew how. A native girl was coaxed to perform, and when she received warm applause after her first number, the "emcee" thanked her and asked in a professional manner, "And where did the young lady learn to play so beautifully?"

He left himself wide open, for the girl replied, "The Americans taught me!"

Another time at the school, Cynthia said, the Jap master of ceremonies gave a "news" talk in which he claimed that the invincible Sons of Heaven had already captured Australia, New Guinea, Wake, Midway, and Mare Island. A Chamorro who happened to know the location of Mare Island held up his hand and asked, "Have you taken California yet?"

"No," admitted the newscaster. "We will get California next month!"

Juan Duenas repeated rumors he'd heard about me. I'd been seen at entirely opposite ends of the island at exactly the same hour. One native woman said I was armed with a machine gun. Another said she'd seen me running across the road in the Piti District and that I had no weapons at all. A rancher told Juan that the Japs had finally got me —they had slipped up behind me as I slept in the bush and beheaded me.

"I said," Juan told us, " 'what a sad thing our American friend is dead,' then came home and brought the corpse his rice!"

We all laughed, and then Sus Quitugua spoke seriously.

"The Japs hear those rumors, too. They can't stand to have you outsmart them for so long. They're trying something new, right now."

He displayed a sheet of paper on which was written a proclamation in both English and Chamorro. It read:

NOTICE

All service personnel and also all Americans who are still at large should give themselves up as soon as possible in order to receive decent treatment. It is true that by not giving themselves up at once causes great inconvenience to the people at large and furthermore by failing to present themselves at the specified date severe punishment will be inflicted, hence they should give themselves up for their own good.

(Signed)   CIVIL ADMINISTRATION.

"Civil Administration, eh?" I laughed. "Our good friends Shinohara, Shimizu, and the Jap police!"

"Do you believe there's a chance of getting 'decent' treatment from the Japs?" asked Juan.

"Hell, no!" I snorted. "Not after what that Jap officer told Vicente Aguon. We've given them the slip too many times, that's all. This would be the easiest way I can think of to save them a lot of trouble. It's a noose I'm not sticking my neck into!"

"Well, here's something else for you," Sus announced, handing me another sheet.

It was a typewritten list which he had somehow obtained from the Japs, showing the total casualties for American navy men at Guam. It listed the number dead, missing, and in hospital. My name was on the list of those missing, as were those of Krump, Johnston, Jones, Yablonsky, and

Tyson. They knew all about all of us, all right, no doubt about that.

Inevitably, the talk turned to the latest atrocity stories. Japs and natives of Saipan had hidden along the Barrigada Road, leapt out on a Chamorro riding by on a bicycle, and for no reason at all beaten him unmercifully. A girl who refused to bow before the emperor's picture was knocked down by an irate Japanese colonel who kicked her and stamped on her, crippling her for life.

And, as usual, there was an atrocity story about a native tortured in an attempt to get information about me. Such barbarisms were happening more and more often, they said. This time the sufferer was a native who had worked around the Communication Office and who had no idea at all where I might be. Someone reported to the Japs that he knew me, and a patrol had come out and taken him in for questioning. When he denied knowing my whereabouts, they beat him with a bull whip until his back was cut to bloody strips. He fainted. They gave him time to recuperate and resumed grilling him. He still couldn't tell them anything, and again they almost killed him with the whip. He was still in jail.

Hearing this made me feel sick. This native was a kind, likable fellow. Was it right for me to remain in hiding and cause so much suffering to these people? Wouldn't it be better to give myself up?

As if she were reading my thoughts, Mrs. Johnston rose and said, "Mr. Tweed, I'd like to talk to you a few minutes alone."

We went out on the porch.

"Never give up," she whispered. "Never give up, no matter what happens."

"I can't stand to think of what others have to go through to keep me alive," I said.

"I know," she went on, "but you have much more to fight for than your own existence. The people of Guam feel that as long as you hold out the Americans will come back. If you surrender, they will believe you have lost your faith and think the Japs have won. They will give up hope."

Mrs. Johnston's words made a deep impression. Without them I would have surrendered, sooner or later, even though it meant my execution. I couldn't have let my friends go on being tortured for my sake. Mrs. Johnston had put my struggle for life in an entirely new light. Now I saw myself as a part of a cause much bigger than myself. Then and there I resolved never to betray the confidence that the people of Guam had in America.

9

SUS QUITUGUA came over to my cave one evening and said, "I've heard where Tyson is. How'd you like to go and see him?"

"I'd like it fine," I said, and we got Sus Mesa to take us in his jitney to Pago, several miles down the road toward Agaña, where a fellow named Tony was taking care of Al.

It was after ten o'clock when we pulled in at Tony's ranch, and the house was dark. We roused them, and Al, cleanshaven and looking very well, came out from where he'd been sleeping in the back room.

"Ray! You old son-of-a-gun! It's swell to see you!"

We shook hands warmly and Al brought me up to date on what had happened to him.

"That night after I left you I got so damn tired of dragging that rubber shoe that I crawled into a clump of shrubs near the road and went to sleep. I woke up in broad daylight—in full view of a couple of bull carts passing by. I slipped across the road and asked at a ranch house for water."

"Boy! You were taking some chance!"

"Yeah, but it was the luckiest move I ever made. They brought me out here to Tony."

Tony's brown face lit up with pleasure. "We're glad to be able to help Tyson," he said. "If the Japs come out here, I'll take to the bush with him myself. I know my way around, and we'll give them more of a chase than they ask for."

I went home feeling that Al was in excellent hands.

My own situation, however, was not the best. My relations with Manuel had never been on a footing that I completely understood. I never knew what he'd do next. He seemed pleased to have me staying at his ranch, yet his words to me, always prefaced with "Hey!" or "Here!" were usually far from friendly.

The incident of the oranges had given me a jolt. I'd begun to study this man who held my life in his hands. I soon learned that he was very ambitious. Before the war he'd been an assemblyman for Yoña District. Although the Guam Assembly and Guam Council had no judicial or legislative powers, they met in regular sessions and acted in an advisory capacity to the Governor. Being an assemblyman had given Manuel the prestige that he craved. Everything that he did was pointed to this goal of becoming a power in Guam. He had some six hundred chickens—twice as many as most of the people in the district. He grew more corn than he needed so that when a neighbor ran out he'd have to come to Manuel for help. The corn he sold for ten cents a pound, a high price. Manuel was always boasting that he had coffee cans filled with both American and Japanese money.

I came to the conclusion that Manuel risked hiding me in order to satisfy his insatiable desire to be regarded as a man of consequence. It made him a "big shot" to have an American dependent on him for his life. After I had been there about a month, Pedro told me that Manuel had been the Chamorro leader of the searching party at Manengon and that it was he who had turned over to the Japs the piece of khaki cloth that Jones had left behind. He had heard that the Americans in the bushes had a list of Jap collaborators, and he wanted to get off that list.

On the first day I entered the cave, I said to Manuel, "Let's keep this hiding place a secret. Please don't bring anybody here."

"Okay, nobody know nothing," he agreed.

Two days later he brought in three friends, natives who were complete strangers to me. He neither greeted me nor introduced the newcomers.

"Here he is," Manuel informed them, waving a hand in my direction. "I keep him here. I feed him."

Two or three times every week he brought in strangers, showing off the American, although he knew that if word of his hiding me reached the Japs it meant the bull whip for him and execution for me. He often belittled me before the visitors to show that he was master of the situation. Once when he came in with two friends, I had a small fire sending up smoke to drive out mosquitoes. Manuel strode over and kicked the embers apart, saying, "What da hell, fire! You no need! Somebody see smoke!"

On his next visit, also with companions, I had no fire. The mosquitoes started biting him. He looked at me angrily and snapped, "Whassamatta you? Too lazy build fire keep out mosquitoes?"

I replied nothing. My hands were tied. I could not quarrel with the man who was feeding me.

One day after I'd been there about two months, Manuel came running in breathlessly. For once he was alone.

"Japs on way!" he puffed. "You gotta leave!"

"Wait a second. Who told you?"

He named the wife of a half-breed Jap. "She say they comin' here!"

I questioned him further and found that by "here" he didn't mean the cave or his farm, but the district. And they weren't actually on the way; they were just planning to search. They'd gone over this section once. I thought it was unlikely that they'd return so soon.

"I don't believe they're coming back, Manuel. They've put out this word as a trick. That Jap's wife is probably in cahoots with them. Now they'll set sentries on the roads to catch anybody who falls for their trap and tries to move. Don't you think it would be better if I stayed?"

"Mebbe you right. Okay, this time," he agreed reluctantly.

The next day we heard that Jap sailors with rifles were patrolling the highway.

Manuel was still nervous. When he suggested that he knew a good place for me in the mountains, I couldn't refuse to go.

It was May 24, 1942, that we trudged three miles into the mountains back of Yoña to a deserted grass-thatched shack.

"I bring food every day," Manuel promised as he left.

I had nothing with me but a few cans of food, a gallon of water, some extra clothing, and my bedding.

During the next week Manuel came twice, each time bringing food for no more than one meal. In between his visits I went hungry. Luckily, a stream ran down the near-by canyon.

Besides hunger, I had mosquitoes to fight. It was hot weather, and they were so thick you could cut through clouds of them with a knife. Inside the shack I had to keep three fires burning to send up enough smoke to drive the pests away. They stabbed me all through the night whenever one of the fires died down. I was up and down every hour, tending those damn fires.

One morning an old man named José Mendiola, who lived on the ranch up above me, taking care of some pigs and cattle for Manuel, wandered down to see me. He invited me to sleep at his house that night. I explained that I'd better not go up there, since doing so would endanger both him and me.

"Nobody see you. Too far back in the hills," he insisted.

Still I refused.

"No mosquitoes," he added as a last inducement.

The words were hardly out of his mouth before I said, "Let's go!"

José, his wife, and his son were as hospitable as they could be. While they slept on strips of bamboo on the floor, I had a canvas army cot, a blanket over me, and a kapok pillow for my head. Unmolested by mosquitoes in the higher, drier altitude, I went to bed at nine and slept soundly until six the next morning.

For breakfast, we had fried eggs, milk, and corn pie made of ground meal mixed with coconut milk and fried on top of the stove like hot cakes. As I wolfed them down, I thought how much Jones, who was a Southerner, liked them.

The next time Manuel came up, I mentioned that José
had visited me, not expecting the storm that followed.

"I no say he can come! That old fool!" shouted Manuel,
and he marched up to the poor old man's house in a huff,
and must have told him not to see me again, for he
never came back. I felt sorry for José. He'd only wanted
to be friendly to someone in trouble. I was left alone again.

I was soon without anything at all to eat. Some squash
that had been planted around the house had spread into
thick beds of vines, but there were no squash on them. I'd
heard of people eating the tips of pumpkin vines, and so I
picked the tender shoots of the squash and boiled them.
I found I could eat them all right, and I drank the water in
which they were cooked, but the shoots were all gone with
that one meal. I then tried boiling the vines, but they
were tough and tasteless as weeds. I couldn't get them
down.

I had never been so hungry as I was then. Manuel had
said, "I come tomorrow," but he didn't show up. The first
thirty-six hours after I ate the squash tips were the worst.
I foraged through the woods for anything I could find. Although I didn't want to eat betel nuts, because I knew
they had a narcotic effect, I tried them anyway. They
were so acrid they drew my mouth up in a knot. I husked
a *pajun* nut, chopped it in half, and lifted out a kernel about
the size of the end of my forefinger. I bit down on it, but
it wasn't ripe and tasted bitter as a peach pit. In despera-
tion, I waded in the mountain stream trying to catch some
tiny shrimp there, but never was able to get near one.

All I could do was starve it out, waiting for Manuel. It
was four days after I'd eaten the squash tips that he showed
up, bringing a visitor whom I recognized. It was Laurenzo

Siguenza, an active collaborator with the Japs. Before the war, he'd worked at the United States Agricultural Station, and my friends had told me he was now questioning the natives hauled in by the Jap searching parties. He had grilled Manuel Aguon.

If I'd been in the cave, well-fed, and comfortable, instead of stomach shrunken from four days' starvation on that mosquito-infested ranch, I probably wouldn't have said anything to betray my feelings. But as it was, I blew up.

"It's a good thing you didn't come here alone, Siguenza!" I said. "If you had, you never would have left here alive, you lousy traitor!"

He began trying to make excuses for his help to the Japs.

"It's too late a date for you to try to weasel out. You're on my list, and you're on other lists. When the Americans come back, you're finished!"

"I can explain everything," he said uncertainly.

"You won't have a chance to explain," I retorted.

Siguenza looked frightened.

As my anger subsided, I realized that I was taking a heluva chance. What was to keep Siguenza from handing me over to the Japs? I thought I'd better be sure that the scare had "taken" sufficiently to knock any such idea clear out of his head.

I strode over to him. "Maybe you think you can go down to Agaña and tell your friends the Japs where I am."

His face reddened as if I'd guessed his thoughts.

"But remember this," I warned him, "the Japs have tried before and haven't caught me yet. Chances are I can get away once more. And I promise you that if you send them here and they *don't* get me, *I'll certainly get you!*" I put my hand on my pistol butt.

Sweat popped out on his forehead. "I'd never think of turning you in!" he protested. "Never think of it for a minute!"

I thought he sounded thoroughly intimidated.

"The Japs made him. . . ." Manuel began, apologizing for the traitor. I'd had all I could take from Manuel. I doubled up my fist, walked over to him, and said between my teeth, "Shut up, Manuel! One more word and I'll let you have it!"

This was the end of my period of compromise. I wanted no more help from Manuel Cruz.

As the pair hurried single file down the path away from the shack, I laughed at myself for my audacity. I had some nerve, telling them off, when they could easily report me to the Japs. Yet I realized that in anger I'd spoken the confidence I'd come to feel. I'd survived for over three months and so had the other Americans. The Chamorros were giving priceless help, and I was learning my way around in the bush. I believed I could at least give the Japs a run for their money.

Now it was time to get out.

PART TWO

THE HAVEN

10

IN A few days, I was comfortably settled in a place which I liked better than any other I'd found. My friend Limtiaco had slipped me clear across the island to Tumon, north of Agaña, where two brothers, Juan and Joaquín Flores, had built a special shelter for me across the road from Joaquín's ranch. They'd spared no trouble to make it sturdy and livable. It had a board floor, eight by eight, with sides of plaited coconut fronds and a water-tight tarpaulin roof.

It was completely surrounded by bushes so thick it was impossible to see more than a few feet. If planes came over, I wasn't able to see them unless they flew directly over my head.

Food was brought to me by three friends—Limty, Tommy Tanaka, or Félix Torres, brother of "Walker's Deluxe Joe" Torres. They couldn't have taken better care of me if I'd been a prize fighting cock. For breakfast I ate bacon and eggs or hot cakes with *tuba* syrup. For lunch and dinner I frequently had chicken, beefsteak, or pork chops. I had an ever-increasing store of forty-odd varieties of canned goods from sweet and dill pickles to peas and corned beef.

At one time I had eighty cans, most of them contributed by Tommy Tanaka and generous, loyal Mrs. Dejima.

Behind my shelter, I had a small canvas lean-to where I cooked my meals. Three stones around the fire supported my kettle or frying pan. I had all the basic ingredients for "setting a good table"—flour, baking powder, salt, pepper, sugar, eggs, and rice.

Joaquín brought half a gasoline drum in which I caught rainwater from the roof to use for drinking and bathing. In rainy weather, I could take all the baths I wanted. During the dry spells, I conserved water and bathed as little as possible, for Joaquín was good enough to cart my bath water over from his place in gallon jugs.

The fellows brought all my gear over, and so I set up the radio and got the paper out again. The most exciting news now was from Russia, Australia, and Africa. The Germans had stormed the gates of Moscow and had been stopped in their tracks. American planes were bombing the Japs in the Pacific, but Bataan and Corregidor had fallen and the Voice of Freedom had gone off the air. It didn't look as if the United States Navy would get around to Guam for quite a while.

Joaquín, like Juan Cruz, was one of those agreeable fellows who took everything in his stride and was always smiling. He came over to see me almost every day and as we sat and talked, drinking *tuba* together, we became good friends.

"Joaquín, teach me some Chamorro," I asked him once.

"Sure," he replied, and rattled off a string of sentences so fast I couldn't tell where one word ended and the next began.

The next day he asked me if I remembered what he'd

"taught" me. When I had to confess I didn't, he joked, "Oh, your head's no good!"

About a week after I got settled, I had a surprise visit from Tonie. The folks at Juan Cruz's place had heard from Limty where I was, and Tonie had walked the whole ten miles over rough back trails to get there. She carried with her presents from the Cruz family—a basketful of vegetables, a live chicken, and about a ten-pound watermelon! How she had ever been able to make it, I don't know.

Nobody who ever came to see me cheered me up as much as that girl did. Almost everybody wanted to help me because I was an American, but Tonie liked me. She worried about my having to sleep outdoors so much, about whether I was getting enough to eat, and asked if I had medicine in case I got sick. I told her not to worry about me but to be more careful about herself. She'd have had a tough time explaining to the Japs where she was going with all that food. When she left, I asked her to come again, but not to carry anything that might arouse suspicions and get her into trouble with the Japs.

The next time she came to visit me she brought me what proved to be, next to my pistol, my most treasured possession—a mosquito net. It was large enough so that I could get inside, lie down and stretch out. No longer would I have to get up at all hours of the night to drive away the mosquitoes by replenishing my fire. In daylight, when it was too dangerous to build a fire, I could spend part of the time inside it.

I was so deeply grateful for the gift that I wanted to pay her for it. The next time Limty came out I borrowed ten yen from him which I tried to give to Tonie on her next visit. She steadfastly refused to accept the money, saying that she had given the net to me as a gift.

I was in such a good spot that I wanted the few who knew where I was to be especially closemouthed. I pleaded with them not to bring even my best friends there, or to mention my name to a soul. Joaquín and Tommy were very careful, but Limty and Juan brought someone along nearly every time they came. They didn't do it to show me off as if I were an animal in a cage, as Manuel had done, but just to do their friends a favor.

Each time after a new visitor left, I begged the one who'd brought him not to keep it up. Once when Juan had led in some new guest, he smiled apologetically and said, "Okay, you can just wait and bawl me out next time I come."

I couldn't stay angry with these fellows, but it was breaking my heart to see our security unravel before my eyes.

Limty brought in Felix Torres, who said he thought he could get me a better typewriter through his cousin José Torres.

"Where does your cousin work?" I asked.

"For Tomás Oka."

Oka, Commissioner of Sinajaña District, and a half-breed Jap, was a full-fledged collaborator, the only Commissioner in Guam permitted to carry a gun.

"For God's sake, don't mention my name to your cousin if he works for Oka!" I exclaimed. "Just forget about the typewriter."

The number of persons who knew where I was kept increasing until finally I counted twenty-six who either knew my hideout or had actually been there and seen me. Common sense told me that one of these might talk and the Japs learn of my location at any time.

One day as I sat at the table, I heard what sounded like a cow mooing outside. After it was repeated several times, I realized that it was someone imitating the sound, as natives do when searching for their animals.

I hoped that whoever it was wouldn't happen on my shelter. I watched the trail leading to my place, and finally a grown boy appeared. He approached to within forty feet before he saw my hut, it was so well concealed in the bush. He stopped, astonished, staring, then turned and darted away. I did some fast thinking. Should I let him go? If I did, he'd certainly spread stories about the mysterious little shelter in the wood. But what else could I do? I didn't want to kill anybody not a Jap.

I decided to scare him so badly that he'd be afraid to talk. I grabbed my pistol and ran after him, catching up with him after he'd passed the edge of the wood and entered an open field.

"Hey, you!" I shouted.

He stopped and looked back.

"Come here!" I ordered, pretending to be very angry.

He hesitated.

"Come back, damn it!" I commanded, waving my gun at him.

He came slowly toward me.

"What is your name?" I asked sternly.

"Manuel P. Castro."

"How old are you, Manuel Castro?" I frowned as I questioned him.

"Sixteen."

"What are you doing here?"

"Looking for my cow."

"In looking for your cow, you found something else, didn't you?"

"Yes."

"Now do you think I am going to let you go and tell people you saw me?"

He didn't answer.

"I don't like to kill people, especially young boys, but sometimes I have to," I threatened.

He became so badly frightened that the blood drained from his face.

"Please let me go! I won't tell anybody!" His voice shook.

"Others have promised the same thing, yet as soon as they got away they told," I said, refusing to release him. After keeping him in anguish for about five minutes, I decided he was so badly frightened that he'd follow any instructions I gave him.

"You must swear not to tell your mother, your father, or anyone else that you saw me or where I stay. If you tell even one person, I have friends who will hear of it. Then I will come to your house and kill you."

Finally I said, "You may go!" and he shot down the path as if running from the devil.

Although I was usually extremely cautious, I pulled one foolhardy stunt at this time. One night, Limty and Juan had taken me in Juan's jitney by a back road across the island to visit Juan Cruz and to pick up a bag of canned goods I'd hidden in the bush. After we'd retrieved the food, Juan begged me to drive so he could sleep.

"And don't drive over the back road," he said. "It's too rough. Stay on the main highway and we will make better time."

I protested, "That goes right through Agaña, Jap head-quarters. I can't do that."

"Why not?" he said sleepily. "Only a few Japs are there. Go ahead!"

What a thrill to drive right under their noses! I stepped on the gas. As we approached Agaña, I was thinking that fortunately we had a full tank of gasoline. There was no danger of running out of gas, but I had a moment of panic as I wondered what we'd do if we suddenly had a flat tire, or a blowout just as we reached the center of town.

All the lights were on. I could see Jap sailors walking along the streets with their girls. Our car was open at the sides, with underslung doors and no curtains. I had on dungarees such as the Chamorros wear to work, but my skin shone whiter than any native's. I'd lost my tan since I started hiding in the shadow of the bushes all day. If any of the Jap sailors or shore patrols took one good look in our direction, they could easily detect me.

I had a quick look at my old home when we passed a block away. I'd heard that Jap sailors were living in it, but it hadn't been repaired. I drove slowly to avoid attracting attention. It was good to see the old town again. It didn't seem changed much—shops were open, people were coming from the movies—except for an awful smell everywhere. I'd heard from disgusted natives how the Japs refused to take the time to step into one of the many public rest rooms easily available in the city, but simply used the lawns or parks. The Plaza in the central part of town was constantly befouled. My nose verified what the natives had said. The stench filled the air as far as two miles out of town.

There was no traffic, no cops barred our way, and we were

about to make it through the city when I saw a car approaching on our side of the street. I hugged the right-hand side and he kept coming straight for me. I expected every minute that he'd pull over. We were about to crash head on when it flashed over me that the Japs used left-hand traffic. I was on the wrong side of the street! I swerved the jitney over to the left just in time to avoid a collision.

If some native had seen me that night and reported it to the Japs, it's possible that they wouldn't have believed him. Rumors concerning my whereabouts had increased since the Japs had raised the reward for my capture to 1,000 yen. They were now taking measures to stop the repeating of unfounded stories and had beaten a young Chamorro who said I'd been seen at Piti, below Agaña. It was so fantastic to think I'd show myself on the main street of Agaña that anyone making such an assertion, even though he'd seen me with his own eyes, might well have been flogged to within an inch of his life.

I buzzed through Agaña twice more while I was staying at Tumon. I got so cocky I planned to return to my house and "steal" some of my own things.

Meanwhile the Japs had not been idle. Since I'd disclaimed all interest in a new typewriter if it came from a source even remotely connected with a Jap, Felix Torres had continued his search for one. He was finally successful and brought me one in excellent condition, much better than the one I'd been using. My newspaper, *The Guam Eagle*, took on a refined appearance.

Two days later—on Sunday, August 16, it was—Joaquín was supposed to come over to bring some *tuba*. I thought nothing of it when he failed to show up. But that afternoon, Santiago, a friend of his, arrived with the bad news that Joaquín had been taken by the Japs and thrown in jail the day before.

In spite of my warning, Félix had told his cousin José Torres that he wanted the typewriter for me. He had also told him my approximate location and that Joaquín Flores brought me water and visited me frequently. José had told Oka what he had learned from Felix. Oka had lost no time getting to Jap headquarters with the information.

Santiago said Joaquín had been cutting *tuba* when the Japs roared into his yard in a car. They forced him into the rear seat and beat him all the way to the jail, demanding, "Where is that American you have been feeding?" He insisted that he was innocent, but they said they had "complete information" and wouldn't take a denial.

At the jail they continued the grilling. Joaquín told them that he had all he could do to feed his own family, which was true.

"Your friends have been giving you food for him," they accused.

"If others gave me food, I would give it to my family," he replied.

Then they took a garden hose, forced it down his throat, and turned on the water full blast. When he was nearly drowned, they pulled it out and asked, "Are you ready to tell about the American?" Joaquín still maintained he knew nothing.

Joaquín's brother, Juan, was being tortured in another cell. They brought him out so Joaquín could see what they had done to him. A few minutes later they told him, "You might as well confess. Your brother has told us you were taking care of the American radioman."

"If my brother knows all about it, you had better get your information from him," Joaquín answered quietly. "I don't know what you are talking about."

After another treatment with the hose, Joaquín still refused to talk and was thrown, half-dead, into a cell, Santiago concluded.

"Those God-damned Japs!" I swore. "They'll pay for this!"

"They may be on their way out here right now!" Santiago said.

He and Limty, and Ramón Rojos, who lived near Limty, helped me tear down my shelter, hide the materials, and load my belongings onto a bull cart. We worked feverishly, expecting the Japs at any minute. As soon as we had cleared the place, Santiago lugged in several squashes, burst them open and then called the pigs. They rooted around where the little house had been and muddied it up so no one could tell that it had ever been anything but a pigpen.

We packed the radio and typewriter, along with my binoculars and other stuff, into gunnysacks, and Ramón took them to his ranch. Limty suggested that I head for Sus Reyes' place near Pago. So I settled down in the bushes by the bull-cart trail to wait for darkness. I sat there the rest of the day, heartsick that Joaquín and Juan were undergoing such suffering, and frustrated and angry not to be able to do a damn thing about it. When night came, I struck out across the island.

11

SUS REYES, Deputy Commissioner of the Pago District, had befriended me once before. When the Japs who moved into my house in Agaña threw out a lot of my things to burn, among them were some CREI radio manuals. My former neighbors, knowing I was still at large, picked them up and saved them. Sus had brought them out to me when I was staying at Juan's.

By nine o'clock, I was at Reyes's place, crouching in the shrubbery outside his house and "hoo-oo-ing" native style. He came to the door, peered into the darkness, but hesitated to answer. I called in a low voice and told him who it was. When he came out, I asked him if he had a place for me, but if he didn't, or if he thought it best not to keep me, just to say so.

"No, I'm not scared," he said. "I can't keep you myself, with my house right here on the road, but I know a good place for you."

He took me half a mile away to the house of his good friend, Carlos Salas. "Sure you can stay here," Carlos said. "Come on in. I'll get a mat, and you can sleep in the house tonight."

Next day I sat out in Carlos's cornfield while he and Reyes scouted around and found me a place to myself. It was a small hut on the property of the Santos family—Wen, Frank, John, Agnes, and one other sister.

The shack consisted of poles for framework with strips of bamboo for floor and walls. As usual with these ranch houses, the floor was about three feet off the ground and was not supposed to be walked on but used only for sleeping and storage space. Most of the living was to be done outdoors. Along one end was a bench about six feet long with a wide smooth seat and a slanting high back.

A rectangular yard of smooth bare ground about thirty by fifty feet surrounded the shack. A well-beaten path joined it to Wen's ranch, about a hundred and fifty yards away. On one side, away from Wen's ranch, was a large clump of very thick, high bushes. On the other three sides the yard was enclosed by banana trees which made the hideaway completely invisible until a person was very near. A large cornfield spread out from the banana trees, providing further insulation between me and the outside world.

Of all my new friends, I put most faith in the youngest Santos brother, Wen. He never brought anyone to the hut and he constantly cautioned the others against talking and giving me away. I felt that I could depend on him.

I don't mean to say that I didn't trust the others. It was just that there were too many of them, and in their eagerness to do things for me they worked at cross purposes. I wanted to bring the radio over from Ramón Rojos', and told Reyes we'd have to get the batteries charged before we could set it up again. Reyes made arrangements with Tonorio, a neighbor who worked at the Jap Navy yard, to get them charged there.

When Wen and Frank heard that Tonorio knew I was on their place, they hit the ceiling. They'd quarreled with him over the ownership of a pig. To farmers, the question was an important one, and feelings were bitter on both sides. "He'll report us to the Japs, sure. This is just what he's been looking for. It won't be safe for you to stay here another night!"

I'd been there only two weeks. I took my calendar, and in the square for September 7 put the letters *MFS*, "Moved from Santos."

The Japs were closing in. I'd have to get an entirely new place, start all over again, and not let anyone now helping me know its location. I'd have liked to be absolutely alone, but I had to trust at least one other person in order to obtain food.

Who was that one person I could depend on? I believed it was Tommy Tanaka. He'd told me that if I was ever desperate, he'd take me in on one condition, that no third person knew anything about it. He was a man after my own heart.

But how was I to find him? I didn't know where he lived, and I was determined not to let a soul suspect that I was going to him. This time, it had to be done right.

It seemed hopeless until I thought of Father Scott Calvo, Tommy's priest. I didn't know him, but recalled that one of the prime duties of a priest is to act as a confidant. A man could turn to him when he could trust no one else.

Wen took me to a trail in the bush near the church and brought the father out to me. He was a fine-looking man, his white robe contrasting sharply with his handsome brown face.

"Father, I am in trouble," I began when we were alone.

I told him how close the Japs were on my trail and how desperately I needed shelter and secrecy.

"A man I can trust has offered to take me in, but I don't know where he lives," I explained. "Will you help me?"

"Who is this man?" he asked.

"Before I tell you his name, I want you to promise that you will not mention it to a soul."

"I give you my word the name will never pass my lips," the Father promised solemnly, crossing himself.

"He is Tommy Tanaka."

"I know him well. I will see him after Mass Sunday at San Antonio Church," he assured me. "I will tell him you are waiting for him."

"Please be very careful that no one finds out," I reminded him.

"Trust me. My lips are sealed."

Father Scott then confided that he was helping a native who was also hiding from the Japs and invited me to share his shelter until he could get in touch with Tommy.

I waited while Father Scott went to arrange matters with the other fugitive. This man, José Hernández, and some other natives had one day seen what they thought were United States Air Force planes flying over Guam. The rumor spread that the Americans were returning with an invading army of paratroopers and that the Japs were going to burn all the houses in Agaña before they landed. José had run through town, shouting to the people, "Flee to the hills! The Japs are going to set fire to your homes!" Now the Japs were ready to set fire to José.

Father Scott returned in about fifteen minutes, took me to the hideout, introduced us, and left. No sooner had he gone than José turned to me and opened conversation:

"So you're going to Tommy Tanaka's place?"

I could hardly believe my ears. "Uh, Tommy who?" I stammered.

"Tommy Tanaka."

"Who's that? Sounds like a Jap. I don't like Japs."

"Oh, Tommy's only half Jap. He's a good fellow."

"What makes you think I'm going to his place?" I asked as casually as I could.

"Father Scott just told me," he replied.

I felt as if I had been kicked in the stomach. "If you can't trust a priest, who on earth can you trust?" I asked myself bitterly. I'd heard of priests who had gone to their death rather than reveal a secret, and here I had to pick one who gave me away to the very first person he talked to.

Later Father Scott brought his brother and father to the hideout. In front of them and José, he referred to my going to Tanaka's.

"Father, you promised you would not mention that man's name!" My voice betrayed my bitter disappointment.

"Oh, did I let that slip?" he asked, contritely. "Please don't worry; your secret will not leave this group."

My face flushed, and I bit my lip to hide my chagrin. "It isn't his fault," I kept reminding myself. "He just can't understand the extreme importance of absolute silence about this."

Nevertheless, I couldn't help being depressed. If I went to Tommy's now, we both would probably get into trouble. However, Father Scott had promised that no one in the group would do any talking to outsiders, and so I clutched at that straw.

Father Scott returned from Mass the next day, Sunday,

and told me Tommy would pick me up in his cart at eight
o'clock.

By eight o'clock it was raining hard. José led me through
pitch darkness down a 150-foot cliff, where we clung to
bushes, shrubs and trees, slipping and sliding in the mud.
At the foot, where the trail led into the road to Tumon, we
waited for Tommy.

He didn't come.

"Can you take me up the road and show me where the
path to Tommy's place begins?" I asked when it looked as
if Tommy had decided not to venture out.

"There might be Japs on the road," José objected.

The rain was pouring down, and I doubted that any Japs
would be out in it, but I saw José was scared and didn't
press him.

"Listen, I hear Tommy's horse," José cautioned.

Yes, there was the sound of horse's hoofs clattering along
the *cascajo* road. We moved to the edge of the highway.
Just as we were about to hail Tommy, around a curve from
the opposite direction came a sedan, headlights blazing.
Only Japs rode in cars like that. The stream of light swung
onto the road and we jumped back into the bush. The beam
caught and held Tommy, seated in his horse-drawn two-
wheeled cart.

"Japs!" hissed José. We hugged the rain-soaked bank of
the road as the jitney rattled past. We could have thrown
mud in their eyes. It was a good thing I hadn't insisted that
we strike out down the road.

Tommy wheeled on, and we waited in blinding rain until
he considered it safe enough to return and pick me up.

Once home, he gave me dry clothes and shoes. His wife,

an attractive Chamorro girl, took my mud-covered canvas sneakers and washed them for me.

My first night at Tommy's house was perfect. Screen doors and windows kept out mosquitoes, and the Tanakas boasted twin beds equipped with Beauty Rest mattresses. Sinking down on one, I found it so comfortable that, tired as I was, I wanted to stay awake and enjoy it.

Life on the Beauty Rest mattresses came to a speedy end with Tommy's return from town after my second day with him. As soon as I saw his frightened expression, I knew I was going to have to leave.

"You know Jake Calvo?" he asked, his voice shaking.

"Sure, he worked in the Bank of Guam. Guess he's related to Father Scott, isn't he?" I asked, knowing now what to expect.

"He came into the store today and hung around while I waited on a customer. Then he gave me a big wink and said, 'So Destry Rides Again,' eh?"

That moving picture had just been shown in Agaña, and Jake was letting Tommy know he was on to my latest move.

"Jake runs with a whole gang of fellows. If he knows anything, they know it," Tommy said.

As I hurriedly packed for another emergency move in the night, the things I said about a certain priest won't bear printing.

Tommy arranged for me to stay with a Chamorro friend, Joe Lujan, who lived on a hill that was encircled by a marsh.

After dark, we pedaled down the highway on Tommy's bicycle. I sat on the luggage carrier, clutching half a dozen magazines Tommy had given me.

As we rolled silently along in the darkness I was depressed as hell. Tommy was the most closemouthed of all my

friends. The Japs wouldn't have been likely to suspect him.
If only he and I alone had shared the secret! I felt I'd lost
the safest haven I could have found on Guam.

When we came to the swamp, Tommy slid the bicycle into
the bushes and we struck out, floundering through mud and
water up to our knees. Joe's dogs snarled and barked at us
and refused to let us climb out when we reached the other
side. Tommy shouted for Joe, and he came down and called
off the dogs.

Joe tried to give us a warm welcome, but I could tell he
was really afraid to keep me. In ordinary times, he said,
nobody came to his place because it was so hard to navigate
the swamp, but now people were so hungry they'd wade
through and scour his ranch for coconuts and *fiderico* nuts.
I wasn't safe.

"I want only temporary shelter, Joe. I know another
place I can go after things blow over," I explained, and Joe
felt better. He really wanted to help an American, but
didn't like to get involved for a long period, and I didn't
blame him.

While at Joe's, I stayed in a small chapel, used only when
a Catholic priest from town came out and held Mass there
for a congregation of Joe's family and relatives. The church
was bare except for two tables and a large altar on which a
cross was mounted. I spent most of my time on the floor,
leaning against the wall, reading Tommy's magazines. Joe
brought me food three times a day.

Sunday afternoon three days later, Joe came out to tell me
some bad news. He looked at me hesitantly, as if he didn't
know if I could take it.

"The Japs caught three Americans Saturday," he said
quickly, to get it over with.

I didn't believe it. My mind simply would not accept the idea. So many false rumors had been reported that I did not recognize the truth when I heard it.

"Where would they get three Americans!" I snorted. "The only place there ever were that many was at Manengon, and they left there and went to the hills."

"That's where they caught 'em," Joe replied, "in the hills at night."

Now I was shaken. "Go on, what happened?" My mouth was dry.

"That is all I know about it. I haven't heard any details."

That night I couldn't sleep for worrying.

The next evening Joe came home from town frightened almost to death. "I was having a drink at Tom's bar," he said. "It was full of people. A fellow from the back hollered out to me, 'Lujan! When can I come out to your place and see Tweed?' I'm scared. What if the Japs come here?"

"I know how you feel, Joe. I'm getting out."

Joe sent three of his young boys with two caribao to take me across the swamp and over near Wen's place. Two boys led the way on one caribao, while the third and I, hanging on to my magazines and some canned goods Joe had given me, followed. It was my first ride on one of these slow-motion beasts, and I thought I'd fall off in the swamp. I was perched high on the animal's rear end, and every time he'd take a step I'd lurch way up on one side and down on the other.

Our trail led us right past the home of Concepción Toves, the girl who had cooked for me in Agaña. Lights poured from the open windows and door, and I saw her sitting inside. I called a halt, started to say hello and see how she was making out. Then I thought better of it. Everyone who knew about me seemed to get into trouble. I might cause her to be whipped. We passed on.

As we neared Wen's house, I went up the path and whistled. Wen knew who it was and came out.

"How're things, Wen?" I asked eagerly. "Any trouble?"

"No, all okay."

"Can I come back?"

"Okay with me. Frank's a little nervous."

I stayed the night, and when Frank came over the next day I could see that he was badly scared.

"What do you think about my staying here?" I asked him.

He was too kind to say so, but I saw he thought it would be better if I moved on.

"Look, I'm in a jam, Frank. Let me stay here a few days 'til I can find a new hideout," I asked.

"Okay, we can keep you that long."

Before I moved anywhere, I had to know whether the other fellows had actually been caught and, if so, how it had happened. I couldn't rest until I'd found out. I asked Wen to go to Mrs. Johnston; she'd know if anybody would.

As soon as Wen returned from town, I saw that it was true. He wouldn't have told me, but he knew I'd read it in his face. He spilled out the whole story.

About two weeks previously, the Japs had received information about the Americans at Manengon from Thomas Oka and a girl named Ida Diego. Ida was living with Shimada, the Jap chief of police, and at the same time helping obtain Chamorro girls to be forced into prostitution by the Japs.

Word had reached Manuel Aguon that his district was to be searched again. He wanted to take the Americans back into the hills several miles from his ranch. Since it was too far to carry food to them each day, he killed two pigs and dried the meat. These provisions, together with bedding, mats, and other possessions, making too big a load for the four, Manuel enlisted the aid of his hired man, Felix Jota, whom he trusted, but who was a half Jap.

A few days later the Japs were at Manuel's door. They dragged him to jail, slapping and kicking him, demanding, "Where those American dogs you feeding?" but he never told. Then they got Felix Jota, and, rather than face punishment, he volunteered to lead them to the hiding place.

It was two o'clock in the morning, Saturday, September 12, that the Japs sneaked up on the three Americans, Jones, Yablonsky, and Krump, surrounded them with fixed bayonets and awakened them. Seeing they had no chance to escape, the three surrendered. The Japs asked who besides Manuel had helped them and wanted to know where the other Americans were, but no one answered. Then, thinking they were clever, the Japs told the three men that they could have a few minutes in which to write letters to their wives. When these letters failed to reveal any further clues, Jap strategy ended, and their usual methods began. When torture too had failed, they ordered the Americans to dig their own graves.

It was now about eight o'clock. The three men, their hands tied behind their backs, were forced into a kneeling position. The Japs then stood over them with drawn swords and cut off their heads.

Wen's story left me speechless. It nearly killed me to hear that men I'd known so well had been killed in such a brutal way. I thought of Krump, brave, resourceful man's man—how bitter for him to be taken. But I pitied Jones and Yablonsky even more, for they didn't have the strength Krump had. Poor guys!

Then I got scared. For the first time I actually pictured in my mind what would happen to me if I were caught. The full and complete realization swept over me that if they got me, I, too, would have my head cut off.

In my lowest moment since I'd taken to the bush, I wrote a letter which I hoped would reach my mother if I died. I penciled it on a page from a Jap copybook, crisscrossed with blue lines, each square intended for a Japanese character. Tommy Tanaka had given it to me. I told her that these might be my last words to her, and sent her my warmest love. I folded it carefully, put it in a tightly corked bottle, and buried it, showing Wen where it was, so that if I died he could mail it after the Navy had retaken Guam.

Now the Japs caught Limty and took him to jail because he was a friend of Joaquín. They beat him with lead pipes until his body was purple with bruises. Between beatings they questioned him about me, but he never told a thing.

When Limty was nearly dead, the Japs called his family to come for him, so that he wouldn't die on their hands. His relatives carried him home in a bull cart, treated his bruised body, and nursed him back to life. As soon as he could walk, the Japs took him to jail and started the beatings all over again. Still he never told.

When I heard this, I felt like walking into town and killing as many Japs as I could before they killed me. It wasn't right for me to cause people like Limty and Joaquín to be tortured. I felt ashamed of myself for wanting to save my life.

Then I thought, "What if I do kill half a dozen Japs? When they get me, the fight's over. They've won. The Chamorros will say, 'The American was brave. He killed a

lot of Japs, but they got him.   He wasn't smart enough to
stay out of their way.' "

I wasn't going to let those bastards win out over me.   I'd
have my revenge when the Americans came back.   I lived
for that day.

I took heart, too, from what Mrs. Johnston had told me.
If I gave myself up, it would mean to the natives that I no
longer believed the Americans were coming back, and they
might knuckle under to the Japs.   As long as I held out, the
natives, too, would have hope.

GUAM

★ Shows the location of Tweed's hide-outs and thrilling adventures during his 31 months of eluding the Japanese.

RITIDIAN Pt.

PATI Pt.

20 MACHANAO
18
19
17

YIGO

DEDEDO

Jumon Bay
8
11
7
Agaña Bay
LUAYAO
9 21
AGAÑA
6
ASAN
12
SINAJANA
16
RADIO STATIONS
15
FADIAN Pt.
CABRAS I.
PITI
10 14

OROTE Pt.
SUMAY
RADIO STA.

YONA
Pago Bay
5
1
4 2
13 3
Ylig R.
Ylig Bay

Agat Bay

AGAT

MATA
Jalofofo Bay

FACPI Pt.

N

UMATAC

INARAJAN

MERIZO

OCEAN

COCOS I.

STATUTE MILES
0   2   5

PACIFIC

STEPHEN J. VOORHIES

140

KEY TO NUMBERS ON GUAM MAP

1. Hill where Francisco and Juan brought us food

2. Juan's place

3. Manengon

4. The swamp

5. Cave at Manuel's

6. Mrs. Johnston's home

7. Tumon

8. Joaquín Flores' ranch

9. Joaquín Limtiaco's farm

10. Wen Santos' place

11. Tommy Tanaka's

12. José Lujan's

13. Where Krump, Jones, and Yablonsky were captured

14. Wen Santos'

15. Cave Wen and I found

16. Fadian Point cave

17. Juan Pangalinen's

18. My shelter for twenty-one months

19. Antonio's ranch

20. Where Tyson and Johnston were trapped

21. Ramón Rojos' ranch

22. The two destroyers

12

I LEARNED that in their efforts to uncover people who knew me, the Japs were using Ida Diego and another native girl, Alice Flores, who went from ranch to ranch inquiring for me. Each would go to a different house, carrying a basket of food. "I'm Tweed's girl friend, and I want to give him these things to eat," they'd say.

The two girls had worked in Joe Joe's restaurant before the war. They knew what I looked like for they'd seen me repair the automatic phonograph in the café.

This was a smart trick. I was afraid it might work, and so when Wen came in that night and said he had a good place in mind, it was welcome news.

"Swell, I've got to get out of this district. It's too hot. Where do I go?"

"You know Frank Arbin, Commissioner of Price District?"

"No."

"He's a good man. He won't talk. He lives at Price, right near the school. He owns some land about a mile from the road. It's near the sea, and there are some good caves you could live in. They're near Fadian Point."

I thought it over for a minute. I felt that I could trust

Wen not to talk, so was reluctant to contact anyone else who might not be so discreet.

"Why couldn't I hide there without telling Arbin? Then nobody but you and I would know. We won't tell your brothers."

"Okay. I'll bring you food every day."

That same night I packed up my gear, including a Big Ben Chime alarm clock that Carlos had given me when I offered to repair it for him, and we slipped away without letting anyone hear us. I was to sleep that night in a vacant house at Fadian Point. Wen would come there in the morning and we would look for a cave. We arrived about nine o'clock. The place seemed ideal. It was on a ranch that had belonged to Mrs. Arbin before her marriage and had been deserted ever since. Wen left, and I laid my mat on some bamboo slats on the floor, set up my mosquito netting, took off my holster, and settled for the night.

I was sound asleep at midnight when a terrific "bang!" right outside the door made me jump almost out of my skin. It sounded as if someone had slammed an empty gasoline can with a baseball bat.

I reached for my pistol and lay as quietly as I could there in the dark, motionless, listening for footsteps. I felt my skin crawl.

Then the beam of a flashlight played through the door onto the floor, moved up the wall and across the ceiling. I threw my mosquito netting back. The bamboo slats creaked. The flashlight went out. Whoever it was had heard me getting up and had moved away from the door.

I crept outside, circled the house, sneaked down the trail, but couldn't see nor hear anyone.

I knew it would be impossible to relax in the house after

that, so I picked up my mat, blanket, pillow and mosquito netting and moved three hundred yards back into the bushes. It just wasn't my night, I guess, for within an hour a heavy shower poured down, soaking me and my bed. I sat as patiently as I could until it stopped, then wrung out my blanket, turned the sopping pillow over and went back to sleep.

Wen was to come at nine the next morning. I went to the trail and waited. He was late, and I worried, but at ten o'clock I heard his whistle. I told him someone had come in on me during the night.

"Oh, you had a nightmare!" he laughed.

"No, I didn't, Wen. I saw this flashlight after I was awake."

We went seaward down the hill through a banana grove. We climbed along the base of a vertical cliff about two hundred feet high until we found a dry cave. The ground fell away sharply to a more gradual slope below and was grown over with trees high enough to cut off any view of the spot from below.

"This'll do fine," I said.

"You ought to be plenty safe here," said Wen and left, promising to bring me something to eat every morning at nine.

The cave was so small that when my mosquito netting was strung up over my sleeping mat, the outside corner was out in the rain. I took my food over to a second small cave a few feet away and ate there so that the ants, with which the area was teeming, wouldn't be drawn to my sleeping place.

Once settled, like a cat investigating new surroundings, I got acquainted with the countryside. When Wen came next day, I was able to show him a trail which cut his five-mile trip to three.

Things went along smoothly until Wen began running into people on his way to or from my cave. "I'm going to see my cousin," he'd tell them, but this became an old story, and his ever-present bag of food caused suspicion.

The fact that I was still at large was fresh in everyone's mind. The death of the three Americans was being talked of all over the island. People were saying, "Where do you suppose the others are?"

One morning Wen didn't come. I waited until ten, eleven, and twelve o'clock, and still he hadn't arrived. Had the Japs got him? Were they on their way here right now? At twelve-thirty I packed and was on my way out when Wen showed up.

"Both my sisters got poisoned from *mendioca* flour," he explained. "They were paralyzed, couldn't talk. I had to stay with them."

"We've got to make some other arrangements," I said. "You've met so many people walking such a long way every day that we're in danger. I was scared to death when you didn't show up, and I'd be just as scared if you were late tomorrow. We're not safe."

"Okay, let's contact Frank Arbin."

Wen sought out Arbin alone, and he agreed to keep me. The next day he came to the cave. I was disappointed to see that he had brought another fellow, Juan Perez.

"He's my good friend. He won't talk," Arbin told me when I said that the fewer who knew my whereabouts, the better. "Juan will help bring food. Wen won't have to come all the way over here anymore."

I told Arbin about somebody flashing a light in the house

where I spent my first night on his property. "That was my nephew," he laughed. He told me about seeing you, but you don't need to worry about him. He just didn't want to disturb you—not with that gun beside you!"

Even with the new arrangement, it seemed that every day my general situation grew more dangerous. Wen came over one morning and said, "The Japs have got Sus Reyes. Someone told them that you stayed two nights at his home. Maybe it was those two waitresses posing as your girl friends. They've knocked on almost every door on Guam!"

"Maybe Oka found someone else who would talk." I pondered.

Wen was nervous. He was afraid Sus would break down and talk. It's not every man who can stand Jap torture. Sus didn't know where I was, but he knew two or three people who did. Wen was one of them. How much would they be able to make him tell?

When I saw Arbin, I told him about Sus's capture, and said that it would be better if even Wen didn't know where I was. If the worst came to the worst and they forced him at gun point to take them to my hideout, he wouldn't be able to find it.

"Okay, there's a good cave down near Fadian Point. It's closer to where Juan and I live, too."

The sloping dirt floor of my new cave was packed so hard it felt like concrete. With my machete, I spaded up a strip of dirt about three feet wide across the back, spread it with *fiderico* leaves to serve as a mattress and was pretty comfortable when I'd covered it all with my mat. Juan brought me a box of "mosquito chasers," which made my netting unnecessary.

Mrs. Arbin and Mrs. Perez alternated in preparing my

meals. Once Juan brought me a plate of dessert I didn't recognize because I expected it to be native cooking.

"This is delicious, Juan," I said. "If I were in the States, I would swear it was plum pudding!"

"That's just what it is," he grinned. I knew that Mrs. Perez had been principal of the Dorn Hall School. I decided her specialty must be domestic science.

When I'd finished, Juan tossed me two packs of Chesterfields.

"My God, where'd these come from?" I asked.

"Ambrosio Shimazu sent 'em to you."

Ambrosio was the son of the Jap merchant who'd turned collaborator.

"How is it that Jap knows where I am?"

"Oh, Ambrosio is my good friend. I told him. He won't talk."

There it was again. I doubted if I'd ever find a man who could keep from gossiping, but the damage was done, and I couldn't do much about it.

One morning, as I reached a banana grove near my cave, I heard someone approaching along the trail. I crouched in the grass and saw three natives with gunnysacks come off the path to pick bananas. The tallest walked directly toward me. I hoped he'd turn off to one side, but he came straight on. I got up and ran. He took one look at me and fled the other way. He was frightened, for he began shouting "Hoo-oo! Hoo-oo!" so I'd know his course and we wouldn't run into each other. Wondering which of us had been most scared, I laughed and cut back to the trail leading home.

When I entered, I saw a papaya as big as a football lying in the center of the cave. It had obviously been placed

there to attract my attention. I picked it up and saw that
crude letters had been cut on it with a knife. They were
rather wide apart, had apparently been cut in haste, and I
had a hard time making them out. The writing covered the
whole papaya so that I couldn't tell where the message
began. It took me a half hour to decipher:

RED
KEEP
GOING
DIS
COVE

Then I had what might be called a premonition in reverse.
Instead of heeding the words "discovered, keep going," I got
the perverted notion that Juan might be warning me to stick
close to the cave, that the Japs had found out I was jumping
from place to place and they were watching all trails. So
I stayed there that night intending to find out from Frank
in the morning what it was all about.

Next day, my thirteenth at the cave, nine o'clock came but
no Frank. He was always prompt, knowing I'd worry if he
was late.

Ten o'clock came and I was very nervous. That message—
it must have meant for me to get out.

Eleven o'clock, and I was panicky.

Feverishly, I packed my things. Those I couldn't carry
with me I hid in tall grass some distance away, covering
them over with fallen coconut fronds. I stomped down the
ground where I'd been sleeping, brushed away my tracks
from the entrance, and climbed the cliff, my bag over my
shoulder.

I reached the top, straining my eyes and ears to catch the slightest movement. I'd gone about a hundred feet up the trail when I heard someone coming down it.

I quickly stepped off to the left, but couldn't go far, for whoever was approaching was already close enough to hear me. I squatted behind a thick bush only twenty feet from the trail.

I was hardly settled when I saw a Jap pass on the trail. He was dressed in the round blue cap and khaki shorts of the Jap Navy Patrol, and was carrying a .31 caliber rifle. Two paces behind him came another, and behind him another. I held my breath. The ticking of the clock in my bag sounded to me like rifle fire. As I squatted there, beads of sweat rolling down my neck, I don't know why I automatically counted the Japs as they continued to file past, but I did. There were fifty—all heading directly for the cave which I'd left not one minute before!

As the last one went by, into my mind flashed the picture of the two packs of Ambrosio Shimazu's Chesterfield cigarettes. I waited until I felt the complete patrol had passed, then bolted out through the bushes. I hardly knew where I was going, but found myself on the way to Joaquín Flores'. He was out of jail. He'd suffered and not given me away. I'd go to him. I couldn't ask him to take me in, but I could stay there a day or two until I found a new place.

It was probably ten miles over a rough back trail from Fadian Point across the island to Joaquín's. My bag weighed about sixty pounds. I was stiff from days of idleness in my cave, so that I had struggled on only about an hour before the muscles of my arms, legs, and back were exhausted and painfully sore. My shoes rubbed large blisters on my feet which hurt with every step, and the hard earth made stone bruises on the bottoms of my feet. The blisters on my toes and heels broke and formed again. I was dog-tired but couldn't stop, no matter how much I wanted to. When I finally reached the house at three in the morning, the muscles in my cramped legs were jumping up and down and tying in knots. I staggered to the porch and collapsed, too exhausted to call out. Joaquín heard me fall, and came out.

Two days later he took me in a bull cart to a part of the island where I'd not yet hidden—far up the wild headlands of the northwest coast. Juan Pangalinen took me in. Past fifty, he was a great big fellow with a well-rounded stomach.

He was an old Navy man, retired as machinist's mate first class, and had been drawing a pension of forty-five dollars a month, which was a lot of cash for a Guam farmer. He had his United States citizenship papers and was a patriotic American. He'd remarried after his first wife died. He and his elder son, José, made me feel they were glad to have me there.

It was on my eighth day in a shelter near Pangalinen's ranch that he came running in so wrought up I thought he'd blow his top.

"Searching party headed out our way," he told me. "What if they cripple me? How can I feed my family?" He could hardly speak coherently, and his trembling legs wouldn't support him. He had to sit on the ground to keep from falling. He seemed to be more worried about his family than his own safety.

I tried to quiet his nerves, told him it might be a false alarm, and then asked why he thought the searchers were near.

"I saw tracks where my road runs into the main road."

"How could you tell they were Jap tracks?"

"Because they were small and heavy and had prints of the hobnails they wear in their shoes."

No wonder he was agitated. It looked bad.

Next morning early, he and José came and tore down my shelter.

It was now October 21, 1942. In the past ten months I had lived in eleven different places, not counting one-night stands in rain-soaked cornfields, bushes, and cow pastures.

To add to my despair, the Japs were tightening the net. They had improved their methods. In addition to sending searching parties for a man, they tortured his friends. In place of natives, all-Jap squads stalked the prey. A patrol of fifty was now detailed to do nothing but hunt me down. They'd missed me a few days before less than a minute.

13

I HEADED north. Pangalinen had told me about Antonio Artero. He belonged to one of the best known families on Guam. His father, a Spaniard, had divided his huge estate into ranches of several hundred acres, giving one-quarter, along with a large house, to each of three of his sons. He lived on the fourth ranch with Antonio, who operated a sawmill and raised cattle on the land. Prior to the war Antonio had operated a meat market in Agaña, selling the beef raised on the Artero ranches.

As I made my way through heavily wooded country, I buoyed myself up by repeating what Antonio had said to Pangalinen, "You tell the American who has been getting news from the States that there will always be room for him and his radio on my place."

I was minus my radio, but when I finally made it to his ranch, Antonio, a muscular man of about forty, said without hesitation, "Sure, I'll be glad to help you all I can. I know a place I don't believe anybody could find."

He took me to a temporary tin-roofed shelter. "Wait here. I want Josefa to meet you."

He returned with a pretty Chamorro woman of about

Antonio came up the path from the sawmill.

thirty; she was small, and her smooth complexion was as light as my own.

I must have presented a pitiful picture, long haired, and filthy dirty as I was, for Josefa grasped me by the hand, and tears came to her eyes. "My poor boy. Aren't you suffering terribly?"

I had never felt so welcome in all my life. It was almost like coming home.

I smiled at her and said, "Not right now," and we all laughed. She ran back to the house and returned with a plate of fried chicken and a glass of milk.

"Is there anything else you want?" she asked, as I licked my fingers.

"Do you think I could have a bath?"

She didn't wait for Antonio, but went for the water herself, returning with a three-gallon bucketful. This was luxury, for by that time I'd learned to bathe in one-third of that. Later, we sat in my shelter and talked. Josefa was touched by my account of some of the things that had happened to me since December 10 and assured me that she and Antonio would do everything for me they could.

I'd liked Antonio the minute I saw him. He was so pleasant and so serious at the same time that I thought at last I'd found the perfect friend I needed.

I found him exceedingly discreet. He understood the danger of the situation just as well as I did.

Working for him on the ranch was a young boy of fourteen named Ben, who brought me food. On the second day, Antonio came to my shelter alone and said he was ready to take me to my permanent refuge. He warned that Ben shouldn't be told anything about it.

That evening when Ben brought me some *tuba,* I said, "I

hear this place is under suspicion, and so I've decided to go
back where I came from. I won't see Antonio and his wife
before I go. Will you tell them I appreciate all they've done
for me?"

Early the next morning, before time for Ben or the seven
Artero children to get up, Antonio, with two of his brothers
carrying food and kitchen utensils, and I with my pack set
out for the hiding place which Antonio claimed no one could
find. The route was so devious it would be difficult to draw
a map of it, let alone follow it if you didn't know the way.
We reached the military road, left it, and went westward
half a mile along a little used trail grown up with high
weeds, until we came to an abandoned chicken house—a
shack with a board floor, patched board walls, and a tin roof.

Here the trail fell off downhill toward the sea and became
so narrow and dim that only a person thoroughly familiar
with it could have followed it. At times the decline was so
steep we had to dig our heels into the dirt to keep from
pitching forward. Frequently we had to crawl over large
logs covered with lizards and ants.

Three-quarters of a mile nearer the sea, we came to level
ground and entered a coconut grove heavily overgrown with
high weeds and clumps of thick, low bushes. Passing along
the upper edge, we encountered a series of immense clus-
ters of bamboo, about seventy-five feet apart. This tall
bamboo swayed back and forth in the breeze which blew in
from the ocean and rattled the branches. The strong trunks
rubbed together with loud squeaking noises and occasionally
struck each other with a loud, startling "boom."

The ground now was covered with ten-inch rocks in every
shape imaginable except round or smooth. Many perched

loosely on top of others and would tip over when we stepped on them, making a loud clattering noise.

A couple of hundred yards on—now probably a mile and a half from where we had left the military road—was a crude well. Rocks had been thrown out to form a hole that went below sea level. Cool but brakish water rose and fell in it with the tide of the ocean 160 yards away.

Fifty feet on we left the trail, which Antonio said was sometimes used by fishermen on their way to the sea. We headed right uphill, climbing over jagged lava rocks, concealed by thick bushes and *pajun* trees. Two hundred yards of this rough going brought us face to face with a cliff of solid rock about twelve feet high that went straight up. Following Antonio's directions, I examined the wall closely and found small clefts for footholds. Clinging with fingers and toes, we scaled the cliff to come out on a shelf which took us to the left a short way before the trail again shot straight uphill over more lava rocks for 150 feet. Here we squeezed sideways through a narrow slit between two huge boulders and swung to the left to face another perpendicular cliff taller than the first. I thought Antonio wasn't kidding when he said nobody could stumble on this hiding place. The first toehold was so high that we swung ourselves up to it on the branch of a small tree. Fifteen feet up, the trail swung to the right, ascending very steeply over large rocks for some forty feet, where it ended abruptly in a pocket about four feet across and five feet deep, encircled by an apparently unscalable twenty-five-foot precipice. Antonio, however, climbed first a short way to the left, stepped across the enclosure, inserted his toes into a small crack in the rocks, and worked his way up, clinging to the sides with fingers and toes. We followed, thinking every minute, loaded down as we were, that we'd fall. At the top we clambered out onto a shelf several feet wide which led to a large crevasse. From inside you could see anyone coming up the cliff as soon as his head poked up over the rim of the rock shelf.

The open end of the crevasse faced southwest, the sea lying far below, almost directly to the west. A mass of rock about ten feet high obstructed the view. I climbed up on top of it and came suddenly upon a breath-taking panorama. The cliff dropped straight down toward the valley 300 feet below, giving an uninterrupted sweep of the sea westward, embracing the entire coastline south as far as I could see. Since I was only four miles from the northern tip of the island, I could see most of the west coast for twenty miles. There was Agaña, Adelup Point, Asan, Piti, Sumay, Cabras Island, and Orote Peninsula. While I couldn't actually see ships in the harbor, since Cabras Island blocked my view, I could make out the smoke from ships ascending above the low-lying island.

It was wonderfully quiet with only the distant rumble of the Pacific below, to remind me that someday United States Navy ships would sail in from that horizon. I knew then that some hour every day I'd climb up on that pyramid of rock and scan the sea for those returning ships.

My friends went with me into the crevasse. It was like a great eagle's nest. A six-foot wide, roofless split in the solid rock extended twenty-five feet back from the entrance. The western wall was thirty feet high; the opposite one, forty. We chose a place covered with soft decomposed rock for my mat, arranged my provisions, and the Arteros left, Antonio saying he'd return in one week with more supplies. We'd agreed I could get along all right for that length of time, and besides, Antonio pointed out, the more often he came, the plainer the trail would be.

It was late afternoon, and I was hungry. After dark I made a fire, arranged three stones around it, and fried some eggs and boiled rice. My dessert was newly picked bananas and papaya.

It began to rain. As the crevasse was open to the sky and the sides were of unequal height, both slanting slightly toward the sea, the east wall had a slight overhang, from which the water first dripped and then flowed. My only protection was the Navy hammock Wen had given me. I fastened one side of it to the cliff and stretched the other out to form an awning. While this shunted off part of the rain, it provided only a very small area that was even comparatively dry. I spent the night trying to huddle with my bag of belongings in the small spot under the hammock.

Two days later, while standing up at my lookout about noon, I was surprised to see Antonio's head appear above the cliff near my shelter.

"My friend, I didn't expect to see you for a week," I said.

"I couldn't leave you here alone for a whole week without coming up to see how you are," he replied, smiling, but his expression quickly grew serious, and he told me he had really come to warn me to be more careful than ever and to bring me news that he knew would hurt me very much. He was right. It was the worst he could have brought. The Japs had got Tyson and Johnston. He gave me the whole story.

Juan Duenas, having seen several men from the Yoña District tortured for information concerning me, had decided that it would be better to give all the information he had.

He voluntarily went into town and made a complete report to the little Jap rats implicating Limtiaco; one of his best friends, Carlos Salas; Wen Santos; and several others. Limty, having been temporarily released, asked Duenas, "What did you tell them, Juan? Tell me everything you told them so I will know what to say when they take me back."

"I didn't tell them anything, Limty. They asked me a lot of questions, but I told them I didn't know anything about it. You tell them the same."

The next day Limty was again taken to jail and questioned but without results. He maintained that he knew nothing about me. Then the Japs showed him written statements signed by Juan Duenas which gave the whole story, revealing Limty's part in aiding me and incriminating others.

These statements caused Limty to be put back in jail and punished longer and more severely than any other man who had aided Americans. Juan Duenas' sister, Rafina, was also taken to jail, accused of helping Tyson and Johnston, and was beaten in the face so cruelly that she was permanently blinded in her left eye.

Duenas then went to Carlos Salas and told him that he, Duenas, had voluntarily gone down and given complete information to the Japs, thereby escaping punishment. He strongly advised Carlos to do likewise.

Carlos, accepting Duenas's advice, also went into town and made a complete report to the Japs, also escaping punishment. Then he convinced Wen Santos that since the Japs already knew about his helping me, he had better make a complete report.

Under this pressure, Wen had reported to the Japs, and turned over to them the spare clothing, canned food, binoculars, and other things I'd left there when I moved. Afraid not to come clean, he told about my having gone with Frank Arbin and Juan Perez.

Acting on the information obtained from Wen, the Japs had arrested Frank Arbin and then, after he had left the vague warning for me, Juan Perez. Unable to obtain any information from Frank Arbin even by torture, they then brought up Juan Perez. He could not tell them where I had gone for he did not know. But he said that if they wouldn't punish him, he'd tell them where two other Americans were.

The Japs deputized Juan Perez to arrest his cousin, Frank Perez, who, he had told them, was helping Tyson and Johnston, and to obtain his cooperation in capturing the two Americans.

Juan had gone to his cousin's ranch and told him the purpose of his visit. Frank flatly refused to aid the Japs, saying he would go hide in the bushes himself, and started packing a bag. Juan, trembling with fear, began crying. He said that he would be killed if Frank did not help the Japs catch the Americans. After about two hours of Juan's sobbing and pleading, Frank finally agreed to aid the Japs.

Juan then informed the Japs that he had obtained Frank's cooperation, and about fifty Jap sailors, accompanied by Juan, Frank, and several other Chamorros who had been punished for aiding Americans, went up in the Machanao District, about two miles from my hideout, to the ranch of Tomás Torres. Frank had taken Tyson and Johnston there, and Tommy had agreed to help them.

Arriving about midnight, the Japs surrounded Torres's house while the two cousins appealed to Tommy to betray the Americans. He refused. Juan burst into tears again. "It's their lives or mine," he begged.

Tommy was steadfast. "No, I won't let the Japs have them!" he declared.

Frank made the final decision. "I brought the Americans here," he said to Tommy. "I'm responsible for them, not you. I order you to let the Japs have them."

Torres was a country rancher. Juan was an exschool-teacher, Frank a businessman with considerable prestige on the island. Much against his will, Tommy yielded. He led the patrol through an almost impassable jungle trail, finally pointed to a row of deserted chicken shelters and said, "They're out there." Tyson and Johnston were in the last one. A watchdog was tied to each shelter to keep prowlers away. The Japs forced Tommy to go quietly up and kill each dog. He slipped his hands around their necks, one by one, and choked them to death. Fifty Japs armed with .31 caliber rifles closed in. It was about two o'clock on the morning of October 22, 1942.

A sailor sneaked up to the last chicken house. It consisted merely of a couple of poles and a low tin roof, with no side walls. Johnston was asleep, Tyson standing watch by the fire. The Japs had caught the other Americans by sneaking up at night, surrounding them, and taking them without a fight. That's what they meant to do this time, but since Al was awake, they stole back and waited for him to go to sleep. They waited until after three o'clock, then, fearing that the Americans would have a better chance to get away after daylight, they formed a semicircle around the camp.

At a given signal, all fifty Japs shouted wildly, and one

man fired a shot into the shelter. Tyson instinctively leaped to his feet and darted into the bush.

Johnston jumped up, grabbed his .45, and started shooting. The Japs threw themselves flat on the ground and counted shots until they knew his gun was empty. Then all fifty Japs rose and fired. Johnston was hit once on the side of his cheek, once in the lower jaw, and three times in the chest. Ready to fire again, he was dropped by a Jap bullet through the center of his forehead.

The Japs rushed in and, seeing Al's gun on the ground, became very brave and fanned out to find him. Al had crouched behind a bush, but when he saw he was completely surrounded, he stepped out with both hands up in a vain effort to surrender. They shot him through the head at close range.

As Antonio finished, I felt sick. Johnston and Al had died without a fighting chance, just like the others. Now I was the only American left. I was more determined than ever not to let those sons of bitches get me. I wouldn't leave this cave, I wouldn't see a single soul except Antonio until the island was again free.

14

OCTOBER is a monsoon month on Guam. It rained every day, and bucketfuls of water poured in on me. On his next visit, Antonio sat on my sleeping mat and found himself in a puddle of water.

"You'll get pneumonia," he said. He brought me a large square of rubberized material that he cut from the top of his Graham truck. I wedged bamboo poles across the top of the crevasse at a height of six feet to make a framework, then, using long, slender *nunu* roots for rope, I stretched the hammock and the rubber truck top over it. The only trouble was that it left about fifteen feet still open to the sky. Antonio then, in installments, brought me six sheets of corrugated tin roofing. Three were in pretty good shape, the others were perforated with nail holes. I spent a lot of time plugging them up with scraps of cloth and hot roofing tar. It took four of the sheets to complete the roof of my "bedroom." The other two I used for a roof over my table and "kitchen."

The ground inside the cave retained the water that had poured in, and large rocks, some of them two feet high, were scattered over the innermost section, keeping me from using it. I built a floor of strips of bamboo about two and a half feet off the ground that served two purposes: it kept my bed off the damp earth and made a level floor that avoided the rocks.

I don't know what I would have done without those bamboo trees. I used them for practically everything. I split several large poles and rigged them up into a series of gutters to catch the rain running off my roof. They sluiced the water into a gasoline drum which I'd covered with a white cloth to strain out leaves, dirt, and bugs. A half hour's rain gave me all the water I needed for drinking and washing. I even used bamboo to outline my "back door." There was a break in the wall at the rear end of the cave through which I could climb out over sharp, jagged rocks and look toward the high hill that stood inland.

I was eager to make a number of necessities and improvements, but I could do only one thing at a time. Anyway, it looked as if time was the one thing I had plenty of. What I wanted most was a table and a chair. I was tired of squatting in front of the fire like a savage, at mealtime, reaching into my kettle or frying pan for food. And I wanted to sit and read in a civilized and comfortable position, rather than cross-legged on my mat or with my back against the rock cliff, legs stretched out like ramrods in front of me.

Antonio brought me two boards, ten inches by seven feet. I fashioned four table legs of bamboo, cut holes in two bamboo cross pieces for the boards to rest on, and fitted the legs into them. I slanted the legs so that they braced the table securely against the side of the rock cliff. Then I made a bamboo stool, fitting it together in the same way.

It took me the better part of two days, since I had no nails or any tools except my machete and pocketknife.

The unfinished boards of my table were quite rough, just as they'd come from the sawmill. To get rid of splinters and make the boards smooth, I ground them down with a coarse stone. As I worked, I poured on water, softening the wood and preventing the stone from gumming. When I finished, my tabletop was as smooth as if it had been planed.

The stool was all right for temporary use, but I wanted a chair that would support my back. I cut small sections about three feet long and six inches in diameter from an *ifil*, the hardwood tree most highly prized by the natives for making fine furniture. The wood is yellowish when first cut, then turns rust color, and with time gets as dark as black walnut and takes as fine a polish. Antonio brought me a handsaw, and I cut the limbs lengthwise into short planks. My completed chair had a back high enough to rest my head against.

Having provided myself with bare essentials, I built a cupboard. On top of it, I placed my kettle and frying pan. Inside I kept my fork and spoon, plate, salt, and other small items that I wanted to keep dry.

I liked to sit up until about midnight, but it was too dreary to stay alone in the darkness for so many hours. I made a lamp of an empty oblong sardine can, the corners of which were still covered with tin after the top had been rolled back. In one corner I cut a hole and ran a wick through it. Then I poured coconut oil in the can for fuel, and had quite a decent light. The tin corner prevented the wick from washing down in the oil and drowning the flame. I lit it around seven in the evening and kept it burning until almost twelve every night.

I knew there might be times when I'd have to go out on the trail at night. If I were sure there were no searching parties in the immediate vicinity, I could carry a lantern. I fashioned a crude homemade job. A wick run through a hole in the metal cap into a small medicine jar filled with coconut oil provided the light. My real problem, however, was to give the light protection from the wind so that it wouldn't go out. I fastened the small jar inside a quart-sized tin can in the side of which I cut a window for a large beam of light.

I was haunted by terrifying nightmares which always ended in my being caught by the Japs. One dream in particular remains vividly in my memory. In it the Americans taken prisoner at the beginning of the war were still at Agaña. I wanted to join them inside the big wire-fenced enclosure, but I didn't want to throw away my .45. Just as I was about to enter the open gate which would admit me to my American friends, it shut in my face. I heard mocking laughter behind me. I wheeled about, and there was a native girl, one of the two girls who had been hired to pose as my sweethearts, laughing and pointing me out to the Jap guards.

I was so infuriated that I wanted to kill her. I drew my .45, shot her, then turned and began shooting Japs. I awoke in a cold sweat.

Starting up from my mat after one of these nightmares, I thought, "What if I wake up some night with the Japs standing over me? I won't have a chance. That's how they got all the others. Maybe that's how they'll get me!" I couldn't go back to sleep. For the rest of the night I lay there planning how I'd provide myself with a signal that would warn me if Japs came near.

The narrow trail up the edge of the almost perpendicular cliff was the only approach, and only one person could come up it at a time. If I could work out some kind of alarm system to warn me the moment anyone started up the cliff, I'd have a chance to escape by climbing out the back way.

I took my Big Ben clock apart and fixed it so that the alarm would ring at any time the button was pulled out, regardless of what time it was. I stripped some bark off a *pago* tree, which I knew made dependable cord, for the natives fashioned ropes out of it for their cows. I shredded the bark into strips, dried it, and twisted it into a piece of cord about three hundred feet long. I was two days in the process. Then I attached one end of the stout string to the alarm button and ran it along the ledge of the cliff on the landward side. From there I dropped it to the base of the cliff where the jungle trail to my hiding place ended.

Exactly at that spot was a small tree which anyone would naturally grasp to steady himself as he stepped into the first toehold of the cliff. Several times I tried coming up without using the tree, and decided there wasn't one chance in a thousand that a man would attempt to climb that cliff without grabbing that tree. The top of the tree brushed against the bushes on the cliff ledge, and so I slipped the cord through them and tied it to the tree without fear of its being seen from beneath. I stretched it taut and tied it so that anyone who put even a little weight on the tree would pull it over a few inches out of place. This movement would tighten the cord, pull out the button on the clock, and set off the alarm.

Once I had my system set up, I spent considerable time—
and energy—testing it. Time after time I climbed down
the cliff, gave the tree a tug, then dashed back to see
whether it had sprung the alarm. I couldn't hear the alarm
from the bottom of the cliff. I kept adjusting the cord until
only the slightest pressure on the tree would release the
signal.

Now that the warning system was perfected, it was vitally
important to me to know how much time it gave me to get
up and away. I began another series of ascents, climbing
at a rate which I judged a member of a Jap patrol might
use. If he were sneaking up on me, he wouldn't rush, I figured, but would make his way quietly and deliberately. I
estimated that from the time a Jap put his foot into the
first niche of the cliff until he was in position to corner me,
two minutes and fifty seconds would have elapsed.

Each night before I lay down on my mat to go to sleep,
I put the few articles I wanted close at hand, always in the
same place. If the alarm sounded, I wouldn't have to take
time to scramble into my clothes, for I slept in them. I'd
have only to slip into my shoes, grab my gun and cigarettes,
and get out. I could do all this in less than ten seconds.
After the Japs reached the cave, they would spend at least
a few seconds searching it, I thought, giving me just that
much more time to flee. With this alarm system ready to
give me warning twenty-four hours a day, I felt safer. I
had a fighting chance.

A detailed diary would show that my life had become a
pretty set routine. Each morning I liked to sleep as late as
possible to shorten the day, but I always awoke about 8:30.
The first thing I did was climb to the lookout and search

I went to my lookout the first thing in the morning.

the horizon for ships. I saw plenty of Jap craft—convoys, cargo ships, small escort vessels, and occasionally six or eight little Saipan-to-Guam schooners plying the coast. I'd have given anything for a transmitter so I could have sent out the information I was getting.

I skipped breakfast. I never missed morning coffee, because I have never drunk coffee. A drag on a cigarette was my eye opener. Antonio had brought me a few matches, but to conserve them I usually waited until the sun reached the crevasse about nine, then took the lens from the flashlight and directed the rays onto the end of a cigarette. I could get a light in about thirty seconds. Then I'd drop sparks on tufts of the dry, spongy lining of coconut husks, and, by nursing it along, start the fire I needed to produce a smudge. As the smoke drove the mosquitoes away, the place became livable.

I wasn't very energetic in the mornings. I usually just puttered around until after my noon meal at eleven-thirty or twelve. Then, no matter what the job, I always tried to make it last as long as possible. If I cut bamboo for ten minutes, I cooled off for twenty or thirty.

I made more work for myself by mending all of my clothes and my mosquito netting. I didn't have to worry about darning socks, for I didn't have a single pair left. I had one shirt and two pair of dungaree trousers. I never wore the shirt while sitting around under my roof, but saved it for protection from mosquitoes and thorns when I had to go into the thicket. As holes wore in my shirt and dungarees, Antonio's wife sent up patch cloth and sewing gear. Needles rusted quickly in damp weather, and so I kept them in a little sardine can filled with coconut oil.

I started supper at different times, depending upon what

I had to cook. If the rice was already boiled, preparing a meal was a matter of minutes. If I had *dogdog*, it was twenty minutes; *taro*, forty minutes. If I sat down at the table by six, I could eat, clear the table, and get the dishes done by sunset. Then I'd go up to the lookout for a final check. On clear days at this hour I could see ships on the horizon as far as twenty miles away.

I'd go to bed about midnight.

I bathed and shaved once a week, on Sundays, to be decent when Antonio came. I hoarded the thirty razor blades that Tommy Tanaka had given me. I didn't have any shaving soap, and so I didn't bother to heat water. That weekly shave seemed rather unnecessary, but I kept it up because it made me feel civilized.

The highlight of my week was Antonio's visit. Since the Japs had closed down the churches, he came on Sundays and stayed two or three hours, giving me news he got from his neighbors and his friends in town.

Antonio was eager for the war to be over and the Japs cleared out so that he could get back into his stride again. He'd been doing very well when they came. He'd built a home in Agaña and furnished it with beautifully carved *ifil*-wood furniture. All 450 acres of his father's land was to go to him eventually, along with the sixty head of cattle with which it was stocked.

Since the Japs had taken over, he'd had little time to make any of the improvements he'd planned. Most of his time was spent repairing the barbed-wire fence enclosing the ranch. The Japs stole section after section to use as entanglements on the beaches until Antonio was hard put to it to keep even a single strand all the way around. His

The highlight of my week was Antonio's visit.

cattle would break through, and he'd waste a lot of time rounding them up.

It griped Antonio doubly because after making it as difficult as possible for him to care for his herd, the Japs expected him to provide them with beef. At first they'd paid for the cattle they demanded. But as time went on the stores ran out of merchandise and were never replenished, there was nothing to buy, and the Jap money was useless. People resorted to bartering; a pound of sugar would bring two dozen eggs.

The Japs, passing out paper money as they took the natives' goods, tried to establish faith in the currency. Spokesmen urged the people to save the Jap money, telling them that as soon as the war was over all kinds of fine new goods and materials would flow from Japan's "illustrious" factories to Guam's stores.

Antonio said, "They aren't kidding anybody. We all know that when the war is over the Japs won't even be here!" I laughed, and he said, "Anyway, we're more interested in getting something to eat now, than in embroidered match boxes and straw slippers later on!"

One Sunday, Antonio asked, "Why don't you take off your clothes when you sleep?"

"The ants would eat me alive," I replied.

He came up the next time with a brand-new store-bought surprise—a pair of pale blue pajamas richly embroidered down the front. I couldn't disappoint him by not taking them, but they were too good for my rude cave, and besides I felt that for safety's sake I should sleep in my clothes. I folded the pajamas neatly and laid them in my cupboard to return to Antonio when I left Guam.

That day Antonio told me a story which had spread like

wildfire among the natives, nearly all of whom are inclined
to believe in the supernatural. A Chamorro woman in the
district of Yona had gone into a small store operated by a
Jap named Sudo. She had only three American pennies,

Antonio brought food in woven baskets.

with which she wanted to buy some sugar. The Jap refused
to sell her any, saying American money was no good.

"Maybe American money is no good now," the indignant
woman retorted, "but on the 8th of December it will be good
again, and all the Japs will be killed." Then she marched
out, slamming the door behind her.

Sudo was infuriated. The nerve of her, with only three

cents to spend! He rushed out of the store, intending to turn her over to the Jap authorities.

But Sudo couldn't find her.

"Where did that woman go?" Sudo demanded of a native man leaning against the wall.

"What woman? I didn't see any woman."

"That woman who just came out of the store."

"No woman came out. I'd have seen her."

Sudo summoned the Jap patrol, which searched, but no one was ever found.

Antonio and the other Chamorros liked this story very much. The poetic justice in the thought of the Americans returning on the anniversary of the first Jap bombing of Guam caught their imagination. To them the old lady was a ghostly prophetess, sent to uplift the spirit of the natives. After hearing the tale, I felt a little better myself!

15

NORTHERN Guam is good deer country, and Antonio's brother, José, often went hunting with dogs and a spear, since the Japs had forbidden guns to the natives. Sometimes the barking dogs chased their quarry to a rocky ledge on the coast from which, in a frenzy, they leaped into the sea. One day the yelping of dogs told me the chase was coming close. I crept to the edge of my ledge and peered down. On a jagged point of rock overlooking the sea, I saw a handsome stag poised as if to jump. The dogs did not advance. No hunter followed, and all day the animal was held at bay. At ten o'clock the next morning the deer was still trapped on the rock. I decided that no one was coming and that I'd make the kill myself. I went down with my .45 and climbed out to the point. I raised the automatic; the panic-stricken stag ran right for me. As he leaped over the rough rocks, he made a bobbing, uncertain target. I fired, his knees buckled under him, and he crashed to the ground. The bullet had entered his shoulder, had split, and had punctured his hide in two places where the pieces of lead came out.

I tried to lift the deer to my shoulder, but inactivity had

so weakened me that I couldn't. I sawed off a leg with my pocketknife and tugged the rest of the carcass over to the edge of the cliff and shoved it into the sea.

I had venison twice a day for five days. The leg filled two kettles. I prepared, to go with it, a favorite Chamorro dish, *taro* flavored with coconut. I opened a ripe coconut, poured out the milk, and grated out the meat on the point of my machete. Then I put it in a quart of water and rubbed it between my hands until the water was milky. After removing the coconut, I used the milky water for boiling *taro* that had been cleaned and diced. It was delicious with the deer meat.

I had a lot of time to think about food. Twice a month I had steak—a dividend from the Japs, although they didn't suspect it, as they'd ordered Antonio to kill a cow and deliver it to them every two weeks. Slaughtering day at Antonio's always meant a broiled filet for me. I often had chicken too. Antonio'd bring me a fat hen or frying chicken which I'd fry in coconut oil or boil with rice.

Rice was my staff of life. Antonio brought me a five-gallon, airtight tin, and so I always had plenty of rice, even when I ran out of everything else. I didn't cook it as a vegetable—Guam style—dry, with each grain separate from the others. I liked it as a pudding, cooked with sugar and milk.

Antonio saw a bowl of this mixture one day. "My God, what have you done to this rice!" he exclaimed.

I passed a helping to him.

"No, I don't want any rice like that," he commented.

When I persuaded him to try it, he smacked his lips. "Say, how do you make this? I want to teach my wife!" he exclaimed.

I don't think Josefa shared her husband's enthusiasm for
this foreign dish. He never mentioned it again.

Many people of Guam were hungry. They scoured the
woods for *fiderico* nuts, which were soaked in water to
remove the poison, then ground into flour and made into
bread. Many of them were doing hard work. I heard that
food had become so scarce on the island that many of the
natives were eating only twice a day.

During the food famine an occasional Jap would try to
ingratiate himself with the natives. On one visit, Antonio
told me he'd met one he thought was okay.

"My friend, the only good Jap is a dead Jap."

"No, I think you're wrong about this one."

"Okay, what about him?"

"He came to my house with a couple of blackbirds he'd
shot. He offered them to Josefa.

" 'You keep them, you shot them,' she said.

" 'No!' he said. 'Your kids need them more than I do.'

"Josefa was touched by his kindness and offered him
some eggs.

"He wouldn't take them, telling her to save them for the
kids.

"I think that man is all right," Antonio insisted.

Antonio was ready with the concluding chapter when he
climbed the cliff the following week. He was obviously
angry. "You remember that Jap—the one that gave my
wife the blackbirds?"

"Yeah."

"Well, he came back to my ranch two days ago. He went
past my house. I saw it was the same man and I thought
he was a good fellow so I didn't watch him. He went down
to the bushes where my chicken house is and he killed four

of my laying hens, he killed my best rooster, he stole about
two dozen eggs, and he even stole one of the nests to carry
the eggs in!" Antonio was shouting. "You were right in
your American proverb, 'the only good Japs are dead Japs.'"

As if I hadn't enough worries, my teeth became decayed
and gave me hell. The pain stabbed me day and night.
It was almost intolerable. If a Jap dentist had published a
notice promising to stop the aching, I'd have surrendered.
Antonio brought me some *aguadiente* to kill the pain, but
I was afraid to drug myself with alcohol for fear the Japs
would surprise me.

Then Antonio recalled that a doctor had given his brother
José a purple medicine for his gums. Maybe that would
help. He went to a native nurse at the local hospital and
obtained another bottle for his "brother." It was gentian
violet. Each night I bathed my gums with cotton saturated
in Antonio's "purple medicine." It saved me from going
crazy.

The gentian violet was valuable in another way, too. It
was the ink with which I lettered my calendar. On January 1, 1943, I fashioned a new one of wrapping paper, hand
sewing each sheet. On the outside cover I painstakingly
drew the year numbers and outlined them in mercurochrome red—a strictly medicine-chest accomplishment.

My calendar was an important part of my life. On it, in
abbreviations, I recorded significant events. The one for
1942 was only a small leaflet of the kind usually seen beneath the picture of a beautiful farmerette in very short
overalls, but it became a storehouse of information about
both the past and the future. As each day came and went,
I carefully crossed it off with an X and recorded my data.

From a glance at the pages for September, I could get a

shorthand reminder of the events of the month. The *X* which crossed off the 5, for instance, was marked with an *M* on the left side and a *C* on the right. This meant that on the fifth I moved to Calvo's—Father Scott Calvo. The seventh was marked recording my move to Tanaka's. On the ninth I moved to Lujan's.

September 12, the day Krump, Yablonsky, and Jones were executed, is completely blacked out.

More valuable to me than my record of what had passed was the calendar prediction of things to come. I had calculated the changes of the moon, and drawn little faces and crescents to represent the new moon, first quarter, full moon and last quarter. It was of vital importance to me to know when I could depend on moonlight in case I should have to travel.

The printing job of which I am proudest is the lettering 1944 on the outside cover of the calendar for that year. I traced it from a magazine advertisement for the 1942 Packard. The huge numbers dominated the page, and it was easy to shift the copy and go over the 4 twice.

Working on my calendar one day, I thought, "These dates represent an awful lot of free time for me; why can't I use some of it to advantage? I'd always wanted some time to myself. What had I intended to do with it?"

Quick as a flash, it came to me—to study algebra, of course. As a boy, I'd never mastered the subject, and I needed it to advance myself in radio work. How many times I'd promised myself that if I ever got the time, I'd tackle it again. Now was my chance. It would not only help me pass the time, but would also better prepare me for my return to civilization.

How would I get a textbook? I recalled that Mrs. Johnston had been a schoolteacher. She could probably pick one up for me without causing suspicion. On his next visit I asked Antonio to see about it for me, and a week later he returned with a copy of *First Course in Algebra*, by Shorling and Clark. Mrs. Johnston had sent a dividend, too. Antonio laid a small stack of copybooks on my table.

"We thought it might make it simpler for you if you had a little paper to work the problems on," he smiled.

That algebra book became my Bible. Working undisturbed in my crevasse, I no longer found algebra the bugbear that it once had been. Problems that used to be confusing became clear. I attacked them one by one and worked them out. Binomial theorem, quadratic equations, and determinants became as familiar to me as the transmitters and receivers I knew so well. Algebraic formulas riveted my attention for hours at a time, affording me the complete escape that nothing else did.

I used my new knowledge sooner than I had thought I would. Antonio mentioned one day that his wife and children needed shoes. Every pair had worn out. "My kids run around barefoot, and Josefa spends half her time pulling thorns out of their feet. Those damn Japs have taken every piece of leather on the island."

"Bring me some wood for soles, and I'll try to make some shoes," I told him.

On his next trip, Antonio laid down the butt end of a small tree, about five inches through. The wood was white. I used my handsaw to cut the small log into boards about three-quarters of an inch thick.

I set my shoes on one of the boards and traced around the soles with a pencil. This was my basic style pattern. I then divided the pattern into sections and on the basis of the resulting dimensions worked out an algebraic formula by which I could make any size sole the family needed and still maintain the style of the shoe. I worked out patterns to fit every foot from five to eleven inches long, making twelve patterns in all.

One by one, I cut the penciled patterns out of the boards, using the machete for the first rough shaping and then my pocketknife for more delicate whittling and smoothing. Finally, I fastened a strip of deer hide across the toes. Though lacking heel straps, the finished product made a pair of quite acceptable "go-ahead" shoes.

I passed many pleasant hours cutting out shoes for Antonio's family. I made some for his wife, his eight children, his sister, sister-in-law, and two pairs for his oldest daughter to give to friends. It was good to feel that I could do something, even such a little thing, to show Antonio that I was grateful for all he was doing for me.

About this time Antonio's dogs cornered a deer below my cliff and he asked me to shoot the animal for him. He took the skin to a native tanner and gave me the hide. After that I had plenty of leather for my "customers" and some for myself. I made new uppers for the thick rubber soles of a pair of Philippine shoes. They had had canvas uppers, but the canvas did not last long on those jagged rocks. It was a crude job, but the shoes were fairly comfortable.

One day Antonio brought me a "reward."

"If you can make such good shoes after a first course in algebra, there's no telling what you'll be able to do when you finish these," he grinned and handed me two books on higher algebra and trigonometry. He'd borrowed them from his brother Pascual.

It took me about six weeks to complete my advanced

I made over 20 pair of shoes.

course. These books were my salvation. They gave me the feeling that I wasn't mentally rotting away during the months I spent alone.

Escape was always uppermost in my mind. Sometimes my desire to get away from the island was so intense that I couldn't rest; day and night I schemed and planned. I considered stealing a Jap boat. It was torture to know that there were small seaworthy craft bobbing around in the harbor. If I slipped down at night, there was a chance I might be able to shove off without being caught.

But that way I couldn't take any food and gear. A raft that I'd build right up here'd be better. Then I could get all my supplies ready, cache them down at the beach and set out immediately after dark. I could be five or six miles off shore by morning.

Then I'd head—where? That was the trouble. Where the hell could I go? All islands in anything like reasonable distance—the Marianas, the Carolines, the Marshalls—even those as far away as Wake, were all in Jap hands. My radio'd given me that bad news. I could take only so much food and water. No, damn it, the chances were too slim.

Then the story got started that a submarine was showing up nights off the coast near Merizo, on the southeast coast. It would surface and then turn powerful searchlights on the beach, lighting up the coconut trees as if it were broad daylight. Once, the rumor went, some men came ashore, reconnoitered, and returned.

"Did anybody speak to these men?" I asked Antonio.

"No, they were scared the Japs would see them."

If this were true, why couldn't I go down there, watch at night for that sub, and board her? It seemed like a good chance to escape, but when I considered the number of false rumors I'd heard and the dangers involved in finding a new hiding place in strange territory, 1 gave up the idea.

I had to do something. At least, I could cast a message out to sea in a bottle. I'd heard of the current carrying one all the way to Alaska from Guam. I sat down to write out my communiqué. "I am an American Navy man, Radioman George R. Tweed. I am in a cave 300 feet above the ocean on the west side of the island of Guam, about ten miles north of Agaña. . . ." Oh, hell, I couldn't say that. What if the Japs picked it up? I burned it and started again.

It was okay to say I was on Guam. The Japs knew that already. That'd be progress—just to let a United States ship know that a man was alive here with something valuable to tell. I knew the Navy. What they wouldn't do for information! I'd try to let them know I was on the west side of the island. How could I do it without telling the Japs, too? I worked on it for hours and gave up. But I kept thinking about it as I stretched the deerskin for shoes or ate my lonely meals. Suddenly I had it. I went to the table and wrote, "I don't look to the Rising Sun for my salvation."

I hoped that if it fell into the hands of a smart Navy man, he'd see through the double meaning. Maybe the Japs wouldn't. I added that I had data that might save lives.

I folded the paper and put it in a bottle in which Antonio had brought me *tuba*, but the green glass looked so small that I despaired of anyone's ever seeing it or picking it up if he did. I wouldn't let that stop me, though. I'd make something that would attract attention.

I jointed and fitted sections of bamboo together to make a container shaped like a pyramid about three feet on every

side. This way, no matter how it turned, one side would be
sticking up out of the water or, if not, the triangular construction would cause curiosity. I sealed the bottle with a
blob of hot tar and put it inside the bamboo envelope.

I didn't want the Japs to pick it up offshore near my place,
and so I watched the tide for about two weeks. I estimated
the date on which it would be going out about eight o'clock,
and that night slipped down and launched my communiqué.
By morning, I figured, it should be well out and on its way.

For the next few weeks I had bottles on the brain and
worked up a second plan. This time I'd plant one so the
Japs would be sure to find it. This job couldn't be muffed.
I spent several days cooking it up.

In a long letter addressed to my mother, I said that from
a hiding place above the ocean, I'd seen a lifeboat that had
apparently drifted in from a ship at sea. I made a particular point of this because I didn't want the Japs to think the
natives had supplied me with a boat. I'd rigged up this
lifeboat, I went on, with a bamboo mast and a canvas sail,
equipped it with twenty gallons of water and food for thirty
days, and was shoving off in hopes of reaching Australia.

I wrote that I was making copies of the letter to put in
three different bottles, which, soon after setting sail, I'd drop
at sea in hopes they'd be washed back ashore on Guam for
a native to find, keep until after the war, and mail to her.
Three containers would increase the possibility of the message getting through without being smashed on the reef, I
said. I'd probably be lost at sea, I added, but believed my
chances were as good in that lifeboat as on the island.

I put the letter in an envelope, addressed it and attached
a note "To the One Who Finds This Bottle," asking that
the enclosed be kept and mailed at the proper time.

My real object in planning three copies was that if one were picked up by that rare fellow, the tight-lipped Chamorro, we could plant another. Chances were, however, that he'd share this fine news story, which would eventually reach the Japs. They'd go out and get the note and think I'd gone for good—I hoped!

Antonio took the first bottle to his brother José in town, with instructions to leave it on the beach between Agaña and Piti, a well-populated area. José took it, but was afraid the Japs would see him plant the bottle and could never bring himself to act. Antonio brought it back. I didn't dare throw it out near my place, and so I broke it and destroyed the message.

In the bamboo-enclosed bottle I'd dropped over the cliff earlier, I'd promised the Navy information. By God, I'd have it!

There were lots of things they'd want to know—how many troops were on the island, where they were concentrated, what artillery they had, where heavy batteries were located.

I made more frequent trips to the lookout, taking along pencil and paper. I kept tab on all Jap ships coming into the harbor, the type, number and probable cargo. I noted carefully the model of the planes flying overhead and made as considered estimates as I could as to their number. Daily putting two and two together, I collected a substantial amount of useful data. I'd be ready when the Navy picked up that floating distress signal!

16

ANTONIO kept me informed about the progress of the fifty-man Jap patrol detailed to track me down. Soon after I had left Wen Santos' place, he said, the searchers had come, and, thinking I was hiding in a big field of sword grass, set fire to it. The dry grass burned like straw. Within ten minutes the entire field was black stubble. Nothing alive in it escaped.

The patrol had now worked northward and was searching the ranch of Antonio's brother, ten miles away. Sometimes in thrashing the bush, they startled a deer. One day they chased one over on to Antonio's ranch. I saw them pass below my cliff and heard three shots.

On his next trip up, Antonio brought me a cut of venison. "The Japs shot a deer on my property and gave me a piece of it. Here's half!" he laughed. He enjoyed the idea of my eating a steak from a deer killed by the patrol that was stalking me.

That night I went to sleep hoping the patrol's luck would continue to be confined to deer.

I jumped up half-dazed from my mat at three in the morning at the sound of a loud "brrr—rrr—ing!"

188

"What's that? My God, the alarm! The Japs are coming up the cliff!"

Frantically, I pulled on my shoes, grabbed up my pistol and holster, and shot out into the darkness. I clambered up the cliff, skinning my shins and bruising my hands. Once up, I dashed a hundred yards into the bush and stopped, panting. I waited, listening for sounds of my pursuers. I heard nothing. "They're rifling the den," I thought.

Half an hour went by and nothing happened. Still I waited.

I inched over to the top of the cliff where I could look down into the hiding place. I saw nothing, heard nothing.

I slipped down to the tree at the beginning of the ascent to the cliff ledge. "No one here," I breathed in relief. "It must have been a false alarm."

As soon as it was light, I made an inspection. Where the cord stretched from the bushes to the tree, I found a heavy twig teetering on the cord!

I had only a week to get over that scare when the alarm went off again. It was broad daylight. I dropped my frying pan and scrambled up the cliff. I waited and heard no sounds coming up from below. "It can't be the Japs," I told myself. "They like to sneak up on their victims in the middle of the night." I cautiously edged over to the brink of the cliff, peered down, and saw a shiny black crow perched cockily on the limb of the tree where the cord began!

I certainly wasn't annoyed that I'd had to go through the two "dry runs" for nothing. Far from it, I was tickled to death to know my alarm system worked so well.

As a special favor, I asked Antonio to arrange to get cigarettes for me in town. He, a nonsmoker, thought I was foolish to reveal my whereabouts even to a trusted friend just for a smoke; he just didn't know the importance of this morning drag or the additional pleasure that tobacco brought me during our weekly bull sessions.

A friend sent a few packages, but not enough to keep me well stocked. As my supply dwindled, Antonio got me some from a store in Machanao. He bought all that rationing permitted him and his family, and as none of them smoked, Jap cigarettes piled up in my cupboard. With a hoarder's instinct, I kept close inventory and knew each day exactly how many I had. At one time, I counted almost nineteen hundred. Even so, I smoked sparingly, taking a few puffs from a cigarette, putting it out, and lighting it again half an hour later. This way, I usually got five smokes from one cigarette.

Almost every night I'd try to read myself to sleep. I had nine magazines—one copy of *Omnibook* and two issues each of *Reader's Digest, Collier's, Life,* and *Time,* all of them 1940 and 1941 vintage. Night after night I read them over and over until I'd practically memorized every article and story. I devoured even the ads. At first I found myself re-reading only my favorite pieces. Then I decided to rotate them, keeping them always in the same order. I'd begin with the magazine at the top of the pile and read through to the bottom before coming back to number one. This way, I always had something choice to look forward to.

Omnibook's feature was "Defense of Britain" by Captain Liddell Hart. I read the excerpts over and over again, and the more I read the madder I got. Captain Hart's idea of fighting a war was to keep on the defensive, not to attack. "No wonder the United States hasn't got to Guam," I thought. "They must be following this guy's plan."

I spent many hours at my table, reading.

My favorite article was in *Reader's Digest*. It was "My Most Unforgettable Character" by Stephen Vincent Benét. This indeed unforgettable person was Mr. Benét's father, an ordnance colonel in the regular Army. What I admired about the article was the description of how well the boy and his father got along.

I can think of nothing more tantalizing than to read the middle of a serial on a small island with no possible chance of getting the previous or following installments. My two consecutive issues of *Collier's* carried "Trailtown" by Ernest Haycox, a story of hard-riding, fast-shooting sheriffs and lawbreakers in a Western town. It was a real spellbinder, even though it had no beginning and no end. I used to wonder how the story started and dreamed up all sorts of endings for it. I swore that some day I'd go to a library and find out just how the cowboy got his girl.

The first time I laughed out loud while I was by myself in my cave was in reading the *Omnibook's* condensation of "You Are the Doctor" by Dr. Victor Heiser. He described what happens inside a person when he eats an old-fashioned Christmas dinner. He compared the digestive system to an overworked chemist frantically trying to supply the various fluids demanded during this one meal. When the soup came down, the stomach signaled for an acid. That was quickly followed by large portions of roast turkey, mashed potatoes, sweet pickles, forcing frenzied requests for all kinds of alkalies and juices. About this time would come a shower of ice cold cider to chill the whole system, and all the bells in the laboratory would ring wildly.

I derived some practical help from Dr. Heiser's article. He explained, for instance, that anyone having a disease of the mouth shouldn't aggravate the condition by taking sharp condiments. In spite of the difficulty I'd been having with my teeth and gums, I had been using generous amounts of vinegar, particularly on avocados. When I stopped, my teeth felt better.

Dr. Heiser almost lost me as a reader when he began recommending various forms of exercise. Tennis was one of the best, he said. I agreed, but doubted whether the Jap patrol had brought their tennis racquets. Swimming and golf were recommended, too.

My interest revived when Dr. Heiser explained that in wintry weather when one was confined indoors, setting up exercises are better than no exercise at all. I began some. I raised up on the balls of my feet, lifted my arms, and breathed deep. I touched my toes. I laid on my back and lifted my legs over my head. I twisted sideways, forwards, and backwards to exercise my spine. I cut a pole, placed it between two trees strong enough to hold my weight, and chinned myself ten or fifteen times each day.

Dr. Heiser admitted that these exercises bored him to tears. After I had done them for three weeks, I was in the same boat. I went back to my magazines and books.

One article in the 1940 *Reader's Digest* called "You Can Become Someone—Alone," by Mary Ellen Chase, seemed to be written especially for me. It described the joys of taking a trip alone, chief among them being the chance to relive the past. Many a lonely supper of rice and eggs was made more palatable by recalling hunting expeditions—the hours of waiting in the woods, the coolness and quiet of certain forest spots, and the sudden excitement of startling from cover a coyote or a cougar. I reviewed all my boyhood—backyard horseshoes played with the other boys and trips to the orchard for Oregon apples to be made into tart jellies by my mother and sister. I dug down into my memory and found dozens of friends whose names and faces I'd not recalled for ten or even twenty years. Scenes from my early life came back to me as if I were watching slides flashing on the wall of my rock cliff.

The article went on to say that new acquaintances are more readily available to a person traveling alone than to one already supplied with friends. I had to laugh. It was all too true as far as I was concerned. Fifty other strangers here were doing nothing but trying to put an end to my loneliness.

Ads for automobiles in the 1940 *Life* held me spellbound. Here among the crags of Guam I read for the first time of Packard's decision to change the long-familiar lines of their car and switch to a streamlined design. They presented a full-color photograph of this new Packard "streamlined for luxury." It was the most beautiful car I'd ever seen. My sales reaction couldn't have been better had I been in New York in peacetime, loaded with money. And I thought, "If they're building cars like this in 1941, what'll they have by the time I get back!"

My magazines were frequently splattered with blowing rain. As a result of putting them in the sun to dry, the paper gradually rotted and flaked off, so that every time I read them flecks of paper covered my dungarees like confetti. I had such detailed knowledge of the contents of these few magazines that I realized how much I had been missing before. Ordinarily I read an article once and forgot about it. Now I saw that much of the information in a good article can't be retained by a single hurried reading.

Studying algebra and reading were the extent of my literary activities, except for a letter which I wrote each month addressed to my mother. In it, I told her my condition at the time and described my state of mind.

At times this was pretty low. I had kept setting dates for the Americans to return to Guam—February 22, 1942, April, June, October. As each of these dates came and went with nothing happening to indicate that the Americans were on their way, I became a little more depressed. Finally I had settled on the month of December, 1942. It would be a year since the war started. Surely that would give the Navy plenty of time to get organized and drive the Japs out of Guam. At this time there were only about three hundred Jap Navy men on Guam. It would have been an easy matter for the Americans to take the island. There were no fortifications to resist them.

American submarines were operating in that area of the Pacific. They stopped many ships heading for Saipan, Yap, and other ports, asking what cargo they had aboard. If the answer was "food," and it frequently was, the submarine commander would order the commander of the Jap ship to take the cargo to Guam, warning that the submarine would follow him and if he changed his course he would be sunk. Many ships came to Guam with food that was destined for other Jap ports. The natives learned these facts from crew members on the ships concerned. On one occasion a Jap ship loaded with food and coal was stopped. The American submarine commander forced the Japs to lay to, dump the cargo of coal overboard, then proceed to Guam with the food.

After the Jap ships were unloaded at Guam and proceeded to sea, they were then fair game for the submarines and were sunk without argument.

All this, of course, strengthened my hope and made me

feel that the time was not far off when our surface ships would come there, blast the Japs, and land our own troops. Rumors were started that, had I believed them, would have made the return of the Americans seem imminent. One was that an American plane had flown over Agaña and dropped a note to the Japs, giving them fifteen days to get out of Guam. Soon after the fifteen days had expired and nothing had happened, another rumor went the rounds that a second American plane had flown over Agaña and dropped two Chamorro Navy mess attendants in parachutes with instructions to warn the people to get out of town and hide in the bushes. The Japs, so the rumor went, had captured the two mess attendants and had them in jail.

By now I had learned to accept these rumors with a grain of salt, but I did get Antonio to check up on them, only to learn that they were entirely false.

When December came and went and nothing had happened, I reached the depths of despair. This long delay could mean only one thing—that Germany would be stopped, if not actually defeated, before any major offensive would be made against Japan in the Pacific. This struggle might stretch over a period of several years.

All this, of course, meant that it would be as many years before the Americans would return to Guam. I had only narrowly escaped being caught by the Japs several times, and as time progressed they were prosecuting their search for me more vigorously. Of the six Americans who had remained in the bushes, five had been caught and killed. I was the only one left. Narrow escapes could not continue indefinitely. My turn would come.

I was determined not to be taken alive. I knew what had happened to those who had surrendered. When the Japs came for me, I would much rather shoot it out with them, killing as many as I could before they got me.

With this idea in mind, I placed my gun each night where I could reach it in a fraction of a second. I practiced sleeping lightly, awaking at the slightest unusual noise. This happened many times. A rat would knock a tin can off my table or a night bird would land on my tin roof. I would grab my gun and sit there in the darkness, straining my eyes and ears for the slightest indication of a human presence before opening fire. On several occasions, at midnight I took my gun and climbed down the cliff about a hundred yards where I hid behind a bush a few feet off the trail and sat watching. When daylight arrived, I felt that I was safe and would go back to my shelter and sleep.

After giving up hope of being alive when the Americans came, I was in a much better frame of mind. I set no more dates and so suffered no more disappointments. I felt that it was only a matter of time until I would be caught, but I was determined to postpone that day as long as possible. I lived from day to day.

I kept each letter to a single page, eight and one-half by ten, so that I wouldn't accumulate a big pile. Since I didn't want to keep them in the cabinet where they might fall into Jap hands, I folded the sheets, put them in a dry coconut shell, and hid them outside in the hollow of an *ifil* tree. I showed the place to Antonio. He promised that if the Japs caught me, he'd mail them home when the Americans took Guam and reopened postal service.

The next news Antonio brought didn't lift my morale any.

B. J. Bordallo, a Chamorro, had befriended Krump and the three other Americans at Manengon for a few days at the beginning of the war. The Japs found out about it, but didn't punish him severely at that time, because he hadn't been an active helper.   Now, many months after I had come to Antonio's, someone started a rumor that B.J. had two Americans in hiding at his ranch.   That was impossible, for, to the best of my knowledge, I was the only American left alive.

The Japs went to B.J.'s ranch, where they found his hired hand at the chicken house.

"How many of the white fellows are you feeding?" the Jap leader snapped, hoping to catch the native off guard.

"Nine," the workman answered.

"What do you mean, *nine?*" asked the Jap, amazed.

"We are feeding nine white ones here—eight hens and one rooster!"

B.J. was taken to prison and tortured.

He couldn't give the Japs any information, though, because he didn't have any.

They finally released him, but on one condition—that he report back in twenty days with an American.   If in that time he hadn't found one, it would mean his head.

At the height of the natives' consternation over B.J.'s predicament, Antonio came panting up the cliff with the most frightening announcement yet.

"The Japs got Mrs. Johnston," he shouted.   "She thinks that maybe you should surrender."

At first, I couldn't believe it, but as Antonio told the story, I saw that it could be true.   The Japs had arrested Mrs. Johnston about the same time they had released B.J. They had heard about the party I'd gone to many months before, and accused her of giving another for me recently at a home in the Machanao District.

"No," she protested. "I haven't been in Machanao District since the war started."

This was true, but the Japs never bothered to investigate any of their charges. Anyone, they reasoned, who was in jail must be guilty. They whipped her with a bull whip, but they were never able to force her to say she knew anything about me.

When Antonio saw her, Mrs. Johnston's nerves were shattered. B.J. had just been to see her, pleading for information that might save his life. She took Antonio into the basement where no one could overhear their conversation.

"You had better see Tweed and ask him if he is going to stay in the bush while the rest of us get killed," she panted. "Ask him if he doesn't think he had better come in and surrender. If they whip me again, I don't know whether I can hold my tongue."

Poor woman! I couldn't blame her. I didn't see how she'd been able to take the punishment she had. God, I hated those Japs! There wasn't anything they wouldn't do.

Antonio said he reasoned with Mrs. Johnston. "Tweed has stayed at my place over a year and caused no trouble for anybody," he told her. "All of these rumors about where he is have been started by the people themselves. I don't want to see him get killed just because some folks won't keep their mouths shut."

As he left, Antonio said, "Remember, you gave your solemn oath that you'd never mention my name or Tweed's."

Mrs. Johnston replied, "We're all in this together—but you had better talk to Tweed and see what he wants to do."

Antonio was frightened. He obviously felt, as I did, that poor Mrs. Johnston wouldn't be able to hold up under a repetition of the experience she had undergone.

"Well, Antonio, what do you think? Should I surrender?"

"No, never give yourself up!" he answered. "It's not your fault if people talk."

"Had I better leave here?" I asked.

"That's up to you," he replied slowly, looking at the ground.

This meant I must go. Antonio could never bring himself to say, "You must leave my place."

"Okay, my friend, I'm leaving."

Antonio was afraid for both of us. He wrung his hands. "You're sure to be caught," he said.

"That's the chance I must take." I asked him if he'd deliver a letter to Mrs. Johnston.

"I'm afraid to be seen again at her place. The Japs'll be watching."

"It might stop trouble," I urged.

"Okay, this one time."

When I sat down to write that letter, I knew I was pleading for my life and her safety. If she told the Japs about me, they would probably kill her. I made the strongest entreaty I could. I appealed to her reason and to her emotion.

I reminded her that the Japs were going to be here only a little while longer, perhaps only three or four months at most, a very small span in her entire life. It was much better to bear up under temporary hardships than do something in one minute which she'd regret for the rest of her years.

I knew she was very much in love with her husband, a fine American. "If a certain person very dear to you were here to counsel you," I wrote, "he would advise you as I do now. Your lives together after the war will be one thing if you have remained absolutely loyal to the United States and quite another if you have given in to the Japs."

"I am leaving this place, the safest I have ever known," I ended, "but no matter what happens, I want you to know I am grateful to you for all you have gone through for me."

Antonio went down the cliffside with the letter, and I started packing. I washed my clothes and waited for them to dry. I would leave the next day.

Early in the morning I was hoisting my bag over my shoulder when Antonio rushed in, sweating and puffing.

"Thank God, I got here before you left!" He stopped to catch his breath.

"The Japs are not going to kill B.J. They called him back in and then turned him loose. Mrs. Johnston says she will never mention your name to anyone. She was angry when she read your letter and wanted to answer it, but I wouldn't take it."

Antonio and I were weak with relief. We let Mrs. Johnston continue to think I had moved. It was best for her own sake as well as ours not to worry her by communicating with her again.

The Japs took the heat off B. J. Bordallo. Instead of going to the "underground," as they had thought he would, B.J. had called a public meeting of the Commissioners of Dededo and Machanao to enlist their cooperation in finding me and saving his neck. This open approach convinced the Japs that B.J. knew nothing. They released him after a final thorough beating—apparently for good behavior.

Sometimes Antonio brought me a live rooster which I'd feed on coconut tidbits until time for a chicken dinner. I'd

tie it to a long *pajun* root that had grown down in mid-air
in front of my crevasse and planted itself in the ground. At
first the chickens would go round and round the pole, getting themselves tangled up and shortening the string so
that they didn't get any exercise. I finally severed the root
about three feet from the ground and tied the string to the
nub. Then the chickens could travel in circles to their
hearts' content.

Antonio always brought young roosters, saving his hens
for egg laying. One day he came into the den with a tiny
white Leghorn, just big enough to be taken away from the
old hen. He seemed so intelligent that I grew fond of him
and kept him as a pet. "Biddy" would cock his head and
watch everything I did with his bright beady eyes. He was
soon so tame I turned him loose, and as my frying pan was
only about six inches off the ground, at first he'd leap up
on the edge and peck rice right out of the pan. I taught
him better manners by smacking him on the tail. He would
cluck and cackle angrily—he didn't like it—but he knew why
he had it coming to him. Then I'd put a little rice on the
ground, and he'd behave himself and eat it.

I also had to teach him to stay off the roof—for obvious
reasons. When he got up there, I'd cut at him with a long,
slender bamboo pole. Scared, he'd run across the roof and
drop to the ground. It took a good while to train him to
stay out of my drinking water troughs up there. One time,
however, I caught him full on the tail with the bamboo, and
he went sprawling on the ground. That cured him.

I built a roost for him up underneath the overhang of the
cliff where he wouldn't get rained on. Sometimes when it
started getting dark, he'd hop up there to go to sleep before I'd gone up to my lookout. I liked to wait until the

sun had sunk below the horizon, for then I could look farther out to sea. I'd sit up there after sunset, and Biddy
would look up at me and mince back and forth on his roost.
Finally he couldn't stand to be alone any longer and would
fly off the bar and sprint up to me. I'd put my foot out on
the cliff and he'd jump up on it and then up to my knee.
He'd stay at the lookout until it got so dark that he was
helpless, and I'd have to take him back and put him to bed.

Biddy seemed to like me. When I went to the lookout
in the daytime, he'd come up behind me. If I paid no attention to him, he'd scratch around and pick up a tiny
pebble in his beak and cluck softly as if it were something
delicious for me to eat. He'd throw it down and pick it up
time and again, then make little talking sounds and cock his
head as if to say, "Look at me. I've got a nice worm for
you!"

Biddy was a skinny little fellow. Chickens don't get fat
on coconut and a few grains of rice. He did grow up, however, and one day he flapped his wings and crowed. He
was obviously quite proud of his newly found voice, but I
was sorry to hear it, for it meant that I'd have to get rid of
him. I couldn't afford to have any noise attracting attention to my hideout.

"You'll have to take Biddy back," I said to Antonio.

"No. He's yours. You kill him and cook him!"

"I just couldn't do it. You take him and put him with the
other chickens."

"Okay, I'll fatten him up, Josefa'll cook him, and you can
eat him," he said to tease me.

"If you kill him," I said, "I don't ever want to know
about it."

17

AS TIME went by and I was still at large, the Japs
changed their methods. They tried to entice me
out of the bushes. The Jap governor called the people to a meeting and announced that I was very selfish to
remain in the bushes and force the people to feed me when
food was so scarce in Guam. He forgot to mention that the
near-famine existed because the Japs themselves were taking the food away from the people.

"Pass this word to the American," he shouted. "If he
comes in and surrenders, he will not be killed. He will not
even be put in jail; he will be given the run of the island!"
He concluded his proclamation with, "We only want to have
the radioman where we can see him and talk with him
every day!"

I got his message, but I wasn't feebleminded enough to
fall for it.

Then a Jap Catholic priest who had been imported from
Japan to take over the churches wrote me a letter. Quite
a number of copies were made and given to the District
Commissioners with instructions to circulate them widely
so that whoever was in contact with me would see it and

bring me the information. Antonio saw a copy at his brother-in-law's, Ben Reyes, who was Commissioner of Barrigada District.

In the letter the Jap priest said that he had come to Guam to work for the welfare of the people. He said he had obtained the word of both the military and the civil governments that if I would come in and surrender I wouldn't be killed; I'd be sent to Japan and interned with the other American prisoners. This letter was much more logical than the previous announcement by the Governor, but a trip to Japan was not what I was holding out for.

Needless to say, the letter went unanswered.

Antonio went to town one day and learned that the Japs had tortured Tommy Tanaka until he was more dead than alive. They told him they were going to kill him and probably would have but for Mrs. Dejima. She went to Jap headquarters and told them that they were wasting their energy, that they couldn't get anything useful from Tommy in his condition, that he was just babbling. "Turn him over to me," she said. "I'll nurse him along, find out what he knows, and tell you." They allowed her to take Tommy home.

It was two weeks before he was able to talk. Then Mrs. Dejima figured out about how much of this information the Japs already had from other sources and fed it back to them. She was clever enough to convince the Japs that she'd wrung everything possible out of Tommy.

I didn't sleep that night, thinking of the tortures and dangers my friends were going through for me. Up to this time the Japs had never actually killed anyone for helping Americans, but now they shot a final bolt. They announced they would execute the man who was caught befriending me unless he immediately informed them where I was. When they got no action, they enlarged the threat, saying that in addition to the man, they'd kill his wife and children. Shortly afterward they went even further and included, besides my helper and his family, the Commissioner of the district in which I was found and 100 natives selected at random from that district.

When Antonio spoke of the Japs killing his wife and family, I saw him frightened for the first time. He trembled so he could hardly talk. He said he couldn't eat or sleep, that he felt as if he had a big hard lump in his stomach all day and all night.

"Antonio, you've been my best friend for a long time and you've saved my life over and over again. I can't let you take any further risk. I'd better leave here now and find another place."

"No," he said, "they'll catch you and kill you."

"It's better for me to be killed than you and your whole family."

"No, no," he insisted, "we'll just have to be very careful, that's all."

I had no words to express my gratitude. What could I do to repay him? If I were killed, all the risks he had taken would be for nothing.

One day several months after we heard about the deaths of Krump, Jones, and Yablonsky, Antonio came up with strange news. Ben had seen an American. While Ben was cleaning up around the ranch yard, a man came out of the bushes and asked for some eggs. He was a tall, broad fellow with a heavy beard. He wore a dirty black-billed cap

with the letters *USN* in gold in front, and he carried a
gunnysack and a rifle. His dark-gray zippered shirt was
soaked with sweat.

Fourteen-year-old Ben, scared, told him they didn't have
any eggs. The visitor stopped a few minutes and rested.
As he rose to go he said, "O.K. Remember—don't talk," and
disappeared again into the bush.

Ben was just a youngster, but there was no reason to believe he couldn't tell an American from a native when he
saw one. He said they spoke in English. Who was this
mysterious man? He couldn't be Tyson or Johnston, I felt,
for we'd had an eye-witness account of their murder. Our
information about the other three Americans hadn't been
firsthand. Perhaps the Japs announced that they'd caught
three, but had actually nabbed only two. Or possibly they'd
caught three and one had escaped.

If one were still free, I felt sure it was Krump. He was
the strongest, the most resourceful, and the best woodsman.
It was hard to believe at the time I heard of the capture of
the Americans that the Japs had slipped up on him. To
strengthen the possibility that he might have escaped was
the rumor I'd heard that he'd left the other two and gone
off by himself. Ben's description certainly fitted Krump's
appearance, even to the chief's cap.

Antonio said he found tracks where Ben had talked to the
stranger leading in the direction of Juan Pangalinen's ranch.
I remembered that during my brief stay at Pangalinen's he
mentioned having seen Krump. They'd been friends for
months before the war started. As one was a retired machinist's mate, and the other a chief machinist's mate, they
had much in common. Possibly Krump had gone to seek
help from his friend. Maybe he was at Pangalinen's right

now. I decided that it was important enough for me to make a trip over there to find out.

The Jap patrol hadn't been around for several days, and as it was only a short trip to Pangalinen's ranch, I didn't wait for darkness but sneaked through the bushes, and in about an hour and a half approached his house. Juan's daughter was in the yard washing clothes. I threw a pebble near her and attracted her attention. When she saw my head sticking up out of the bushes, she dashed into the house.

Juan came out. "Oh, I thought it was Krump," he greeted me.

"And I thought Krump'd be here," I said. "I came to see if he wouldn't come over and stay with me. I've got an excellent place—been safely hidden there ever since I left your ranch—and there's plenty of room for two."

"Where's this good place?" Juan wanted to know.

"That's something I don't dare tell anybody."

He seemed annoyed that I wouldn't trust him with my secret.

"You're mistaken. Krump's not here. I haven't seen him," he said.

"That's too bad. I don't think he could find as good a place as mine, and we'd be company for each other. Another thing, if Krump keeps roaming around in this neighborhood, the Japs'll put on extra patrols and we'll both be dead ducks."

"You know," Juan volunteered, "I think you may be worrying for nothing. I don't believe any Americans have been killed."

"I'm afraid you're wrong," I replied. "I've got pretty definite proof that four of us are gone."

"No, no. You wait 'til the Navy comes back. You'll find every American who went to the bush alive and kicking."

I certainly hoped he was right, but I couldn't believe it.

The next news we had of the wanderer was from Pangalinen himself. Antonio said Juan told him that when his nine-year-old daughter had gone to the chicken house she had surprised a man stealing eggs. He was "very big and white," she said. He was barefooted, his clothes in rags, with no hat on his shaggy hair. When he saw her coming, he ran into the bushes.

Again, this sounded to me like a description of Krump. He'd been the most cautious of all of us. He'd insisted upon the most extreme precautions regardless of the hardship they imposed. Perhaps in self-defense he'd broken with everyone and was foraging for himself.

Shortly afterward, a Chamorro who lived a mile to the south complained to the Japs that someone was stealing eggs from his chicken house. He added that one night recently he'd met a native and two Americans on the road. He'd asked them where they were going.

He claimed they answered, "Juan Pangalinen's ranch."

The Japs immediately tore out to Juan's ranch and gave him the third degree.

"The man is a liar!" Juan shouted.

The Japs took him down and let him face the talebearer.

"Are you sure the men you saw were Americans?" Juan demanded.

"Well, it was dark. I couldn't be sure, but I think so."

"You know as well as I do," Juan said, "that no farmer speaks English without some accent. If you couldn't tell after a couple of words whether they were American or not, you're damned stupid!"

The Japs didn't take Juan to jail, but they put a continual guard on duty at his ranch. Since his property was within two and a half miles of my hideout that was bad news for us both.

The Jap patrol of fifty armed sailors showed up at the ranch which belonged to Jesús Artero, Antonio's brother. They accused Sus of hiding me there. He denied it, but he was so frightened that they suspected him of knowing more than he told.

"I've got a big place here. Some bush areas I've never been through. If you want to search I'll show you all the trails," he told them.

"We'll burn him out," the leader of the Jap patrol threatened.

"Go ahead if you want to," Sus said, "but there's not enough gasoline in Guam to burn all these green bushes."

They gave up the idea, but every day they searched a little more of his ranch, until they'd inspected every square yard of it. When they finished, they told Sus that if he saw or heard of me to go to the nearest Jap patrol headquarters and let them know. If they found out that he'd seen me and failed to report it, they'd behead him.

The patrol then enlisted some expert local aid. Villagomez, a native of Saipan, was boss at the jail. He had a partner, a half Italian named Scambulleri who'd worked in the police department in Agaña before the war and who had stayed on and worked for the Japs.

These two initiated searching operations of their own, in addition to the reconnoitering carried on by the regular patrol. I frequently heard of them passing near my lair, and I'd slip up near one of the main trails and lie in ambush, waiting for them to come along so I could end their activities. I had decided that if I threw their bodies into the sea the Japs would not know what had happened to them. I never saw them.

The woods were so full of Japs that Antonio was afraid of stumbling upon one when he brought my food and suggested that he cut down his visits to twice a month. This was the loneliest—and one of the hungriest—periods I spent in all my months of hiding. Antonio's chickens were not laying; there was little meat and few fruits. I felt I'd go crazy if I had to face another grain of rice, but I was forced to dip into my five-gallon can for almost every meal.

I went so long without anyone to talk to that I almost lost my voice. My vocal cords, like my leg muscles, got so little exercise that I was afraid they wouldn't be usable when I really needed them.

I found some relief in playing cards during these long hours. I handled the deck so much that I couldn't shuffle it any more. The cards were so limp that they wouldn't spring back into shape. Depressions were worn where my thumbs rubbed on the edges. When I tried to push the cards together, these blunted edges caught and stuck. The ten of hearts had almost disintegrated. I replaced it by trimming an old photograph—a scenic view of Guam that Antonio gave me—to the size and shape of a card. On it I traced ten hearts, coloring them with mercurochrome. After that, the ten of hearts was the best and stiffest card in the deck. It wasn't completely satisfactory, though, for I could tell several cards away when it was coming up. You can't gamble with a "stacked" deck.

I knew six different kinds of solitaire. Each night when I sat down to play, I began with Number One, played through to Number Six, then went through it all over again.

If I beat old Sol in any version, I omitted that from the second run and played on in hopes of winning all six in one day. It was a rare day when I did.

I played a thousand games of one kind of solitaire. I never knew the name of this particular type, but it's played with seven piles, five cards on each pile, the top card showing. The rest of the cards are face down in the deck. The player turns up one card from the deck at a time. I wanted to see what my chances were of winning and tallied each game carefully. I won once in every eighteen.

Sometimes I wondered what kept me from going crazy with the Japs running by in a continual game of hide and seek while I sat nervously at my table in my rocky crevasse 300 feet above them, playing solitaire, with no one to talk to, little to eat.

I remembered that, as a boy, when I played hide and seek it really wasn't much fun to find such a good place that you held up the game for a long period while the one who was "it" hunted in vain for you. It was no more fun now, but I'd be damned if I was going to shout down to the pack and give myself up. I knew the Japs would never let me in "free."

18

ABOUT December 1, 1943, I realized that Christmas was on its way and that in other parts of the world people would be sitting down to turkey dinners, and I felt a little bit sorry for myself because I didn't expect to fare so well. But when Antonio told me he'd come up on Saturday, Christmas Day, instead of the day after, as he would have according to weekly schedule, which he had resumed, I had an idea that something special was coming up. Sure enough, when Christmas Day rolled around and Antonio arrived, he was loaded down with two large baskets, tied together and swung over his shoulder to leave his hands free. I don't know how he ever made it through the jungle. When he reached the cliff, he began handing out all the things that made a Christmas dinner worth while. He produced a jar of chicken soup, a jar of custard, a plate of Spanish rice, half a roast young chicken stuffed with dressing, a roast leg of fawn, a jar of preserves, a large custard pie, sixteen *taro*, two dozen fresh eggs, three dozen bananas, a bottle of *tuba*, and one of milk.

Then he brought out packages done up in gay Christmas wrappings. I'd forgotten there was such paper. Josefa had

213

sent me a smoking set consisting of a cigarette box, match holder, and ash tray—all the comforts of home! Antonio had given me a straight-edged razor.

I stuffed myself with Christmas dinner every meal for two days in order to eat everything before it spoiled.

Antonio and his family were good Catholics. During Lent, 1944, they ate no meat and consequently brought none to me. I knew there were lots of huge coconut crabs under the near-by rocks. They're land crabs and I decided to catch some for Antonio and his family. I cut notches in the sides of twenty coconuts and tied them among a group of huge rocks about a hundred yards from my shelter. At night I slipped out to the spot with my homemade lantern, caught the crabs that were feasting on the coconut, and tied them up with cord made from the bark of the pago tree. Returning to my shelter, I suspended them in mid-air where they were helpless, fed them coconut until Antonio arrived, and then gave them to him to take home to his family. I kept up my dry-land fishing until one night I stumbled and fell and my lantern went rolling down the hill. I couldn't get it lighted again and had to grope my way back in the dark. It took me almost two hours to cover the 100 yards.

I told Antonio about this, and the next time he came he brought me his powerful electric hunting light. Deer hunting wasn't any good any more he said. So many people had gone after them when food got scarce that José, who used to kill two or three a week, was lucky to find one in three weeks. I was glad to get a light I could really depend on in an emergency.

As time went on, I was more and more grateful to Antonio for all he was doing for me. Something providential had led me to him. I didn't believe there was another person on Guam who could have kept me safe all those months. Nothing I might ever hope to do could repay him, but I got to thinking about how to show my appreciation. One Sunday I said, "Antonio, if I get back to the States, I'm going to pay you for helping me."

"I don't want any pay," he said. "Your getting back to the States will be enough for me."

When I tried to find some way to show my gratitude, I told him I'd send him a money order. He said he'd send it back. I told him I'd deposit some money in a store and he could draw on it for anything he wanted. He said he wouldn't do it, that it would be the same as taking money. I mentioned radios, electric refrigerators, sewing machines, and washing machines, but he wasn't interested. I saw I'd have to use other means.

A few weeks later I began talking about all the back pay that was going to be piled up waiting for me if I finally did get home. I'd probably have five or six thousand dollars, I said, and could spend it for whatever I wanted. He was very interested in helping me decide what I'd do. Suddenly I asked him, "If you had all the money you wanted, what would be the first thing you'd buy?"

He was caught off guard and said, "A four-door Chevrolet sedan." I said nothing, but thought right then, "As soon as I can buy a new four-door Chevrolet sedan and have it shipped to Guam, you'll be driving it in style through the streets of Agaña."

One day I went to the bamboo grove for some poles with which to strengthen the supports of my roof. I'd cut two and was carrying them up the trail on my shoulder when, near the well, I smelled cigarette smoke. "My God, somebody's found me!" I thought. I quickly hid one piece of bamboo in the weeds and the other farther up the trail. As I dropped into the bushes, I thought I heard a native cry "Hoo-ee!" and I suspected I'd been seen. I lay there for over an hour before being sure there was no one around.

A few days later, Juan Mendiola, who before the war had been a bar boy at the Elks Club, staggered over to Antonio's ranch, drunk. He sidled up to Antonio and, in front of the family, said, "I hear you're feeding some roosters—American roosters!"

Antonio pretended not to know what he was talking about.

"Next time you feed them, let me go with you."

Antonio was disturbed, but I thought I knew what to do. I was convinced that although Juan had seen me he'd not recognized me.

"I know Juan," I reassured Antonio. "I'm going to see him and talk to him."

"Do you think you ought to take the chance of leaving the cave?"

"It may be the only way to save my life."

"Okay. Mendiola's staying with José Cruz."

Antonio told me how to get there. Nearing the ranch, I left the trail and approached through the bushes. The sound of chopping told me that someone inside was cutting open a coconut. I threw a pebble, and a lazy hound in the porch yard started barking. In the doorway appeared a Chamorro—but not Mendiola. I lay quite still until he returned to his coconut and the dog to his nap.

I circled around to the trail I thought Mendiola would use returning from town or work. On the way, I saw two men in a cornfield. One was Juan. It was after dark before he returned, and I caught him alone in the house.

"*Maila! Sige mage!* Come! Come here!" I called out in Chamorro from the trail. Juan came out, and I raised up.

"Tweed!" he exclaimed with such surprise in his voice that I knew he hadn't recognized me in the bamboo grove. We squatted on our haunches in the bush and talked. I reminded him of the fate of the other Americans and said, "Juan, you've got me on the spot. There is a gun pointing at me and your finger is on the trigger. It is up to you whether you pull it or not."

"How do you mean?"

"Where were you last Sunday?"

"Joe Cruz and I went to Pugua to get coconut crabs."

"Is that all? Why did you say what you did to Antonio?"

"Oh, you mean about the American? That was a funny thing. We heard a noise like gasoline drums banging on rocks, and I thought it was Americans making a landing. Joe says, 'Maybe we can help by showing the Americans the trail.' We headed for the sea, but nobody was in sight. On the way back we heard a noise up the hill."

"That was me, hiding some bamboo I'd cut."

"If we'd known it was you, I'd have come up to see you. We thought it might be a Marine who'd just landed and he'd shoot us."

"Juan, if you tell anyone what you know about me, I'm finished. I've run so much that I can't run anymore. If I have to leave the place where I am now, I'll certainly be caught. It's up to you."

"Don't you worry. I won't talk," he assured me.

"If you do, the man who owns the land will be killed, and so will I."

"I swear to you I will not tell."

"What about the time you got drunk and talked to Antonio?"

"I don't even remember what I said."

"If you can't remember what you say when you're drunk, Juan, then there's only one thing to do."

"What is that?"

"That's for you not to get drunk again until the Americans retake Guam!"

This drastic proposal astounded him, but he said, "I'll do it. I won't take another drink until the Americans come back!"

"If you stick to that, my friend, when that day comes you and I will go out and go on a drunk that'll make history on this island!"

As the months passed and still no ships appeared on the horizon, I began to miss my radio more than ever. It had been over a year since I had heard anything from the United States. The Japs spread plenty of propaganda, but of course I didn't believe it. Once they sent the story around the island that the Jap and American fleets had met in a knockdown drag-out fight. The Americans had lost 3 battleships, 10 cruisers, 20 destroyers, 350 planes, and 5,700 men. Japanese losses—1 destroyer slightly damaged, 15 planes down, 1 man killed. The natives repeated this account and laughed.

I had no idea what the facts were. For all I knew, the Japs could be in New York or the Americans in Tokyo. What wouldn't I give for just one fifteen-minute broadcast from KGEI? Reception here on this high cliff should be wonderful. I had to get that radio.

When Antonio came again, I broached the subject of my visiting Ramón Rojos at Barrigada, with whom I'd left my radio and other belongings.

"You mustn't go," he answered. "You'll get lost. It's been more than a year since you've been over that trail. Bushes have grown up in some places and been cut down in others."

I resolved to go without telling Antonio until I returned. Then he wouldn't worry. He'd be glad when I came back with the radio and started getting the news from KGEI.

After dark that night I followed the road to Dededo, where Jap headquarters were. As I approached, I walked at a natural, steady gait. I knew that if I changed pace, stopped, or looked back, I'd attract attention. If I kept going, even if I were being watched, I might escape suspicion. I knew it would be fatal to double back or run.

Through the window streamed a bright band of light. A Jap sentry, a sailor, inside the building, got up, walked to the door, and opened it, his heavy shoes sounding "clump, clump" on the wooden floor. From the open door, another square of light streamed across the road right in my path. I didn't want to stop, but neither did I want to be spotlighted in front of the Jap. I halted and drew my .45, waiting to see if he'd seen me. If he came out to the road, I'd let him have it.

The Jap sailor stood in the doorway, peering out into the darkness in my direction. He was dressed in blue denim jacket and shorts. I stood perfectly still, my finger on the trigger. After about a minute, he turned and went back into the house, closing the door.

Just looking at that Jap sentry made me mad. Since I'd already made up my mind to kill him, I moved over to the house and slipped up and looked through the window. He was sitting alone at a table, the side of his face toward me. I brought up my pistol, took deliberate aim right at his head, and tried to remember not to jerk the trigger but to squeeze.

At that moment I came to my senses. "Killing this Jap will cause a lot of trouble. If they don't get me for it, they'll butcher dozens of innocent natives around here trying to find out who did it."

I put my .45 back in its holster and returned to the road.

When I was very near Ramón's house, I missed the trail and stepped off into some dry weeds. He heard them rattling and came out, holding a small torch above his head. I ducked and called softly. He recognized my voice, put out the flame, and came over and shook hands warmly. He took me inside to see his wife. They'd heard nothing from me for so long, she said, that they were afraid I might be dead.

When I told them I'd come for the radio and the other things they'd been keeping for me, Ramón said he was afraid I was due for a disappointment.

The radio was gone for good. Several months before, a native had found the bag of clothing I'd hidden when the Jap patrol almost got me at the cave near Fadian Point. Every article was rotten. He reported it to the Japs, who then thought I might possibly be dead. Limty, who'd been tortured until he was on the verge of insanity, heard this and had an idea. He and Sus Reyes took my radio to a spot near the same cave at Fadian Point, hid it, "found" it, and reported it also to the Japs. They hoped the Japs would declare me dead and leave them alone.

All my CREI books, some of my pictures and papers, my

back copies of the *Guam Eagle,* and my amateur radio-station log, Ramón had been forced to burn. The Japs had caught up with him, too. This was the first I'd known of it. He said they'd taken a leather strap like a fan belt and whipped him across the back of the neck with it. At his second grilling he confessed to having some of my belongings.

"Why didn't you tell us before?" they demanded.

"Because you didn't ask me. From what I've seen, Japanese don't like natives who speak before they're spoken to. What I told you last time I was here was true. What I'm telling you now is true. I thought if you wanted to know about these things you'd ask me."

Ramón made the Japs believe that he'd helped me against his will. When they found some of my clothes, he told them I'd brought them in, pointed a gun at him, and ordered, "Wash these. I'll be back. If you tell anybody, it'll be too bad for you and your family."

Ramón apologized for the fact that the Japs had confiscated my clothes.

"My God," I said, "do you think I care about a few shirts? You've suffered enough without worrying about any of my junk."

"I was able to save a few things that I thought the Japs wouldn't necessarily connect with you."

He brought out about half the pictures I had left in an album—my house, my car with the top blown off by a tornado two years ago, the Governor's palace, some scenic views of Guam. He'd also saved a quiz book, and a book of Rand McNally maps. I was very glad to see these.

I spent the night on Ramón's porch. I'd come twelve miles, and it had been so long since I'd walked any distance that I had huge water blisters on my feet and heels. I just couldn't face the trek home.

Early in the morning I went out to a clump of bushes near by to wait for nightfall before setting out.

Ramón brought me food at noon, and while we were talking we saw Limty feeding his pigs in a pen not far away. It had hurt me deeply when I heard how he'd suffered. I'd have given a great deal to tell him how much I appreciated what he'd done for me, but it would probably just cause him more trouble. If the Japs found out he'd seen me and not reported it, they might kill him next time.

I headed home in the right direction, but a wrong trail brought me almost into the midst of a bunch of Japs who were overseeing some sweating natives build a new airport at Barrigada. As I was there, I decided to pick up what useful military information I could. I moved quietly to within seventy-five feet of the boundary of the airfield, where some Chamorros were excavating rocks, and sat there long enough to get a fair idea of the field's layout and capacity. "Boy, what I'd give for one of the planes parked at the edge of the field." I left when the thought came to me that the Japs might have sentries a few feet outside the circle of light to catch any natives who sneaked into the darkness to rest.

Again I had bad luck with the trail. I doubled back and forth so many times looking for it that I finally had to return to Ramón's house and have him set me right.

By now, I had struggled through the bush for three hours. My blisters broke. I was sore from the trip down from my cave. Every muscle ached.

I made it safely past the Jap post and came out north of Dededo. There on the rough unfinished military road

my legs weakened, and I began to stagger. I had on light
canvas shoes. In the darkness, I stubbed my toes on the
rocks sticking up on the uncompleted highway until my
feet were burning like fire. I staggered like a drunken man.
Looking for landmarks, I saw that I was still miles from
home.

I had to get back by daylight. I'd be a fool to let myself
be seen after all these months of successful hiding. But a
quarter of a mile from the path to Antonio's place, I fell
down every time I stumbled. I sat down and rested for
half an hour. When I tried to get up, my legs were so stiff
that I was worse off than before. I knew I must not rest
again.

Each time I fell it was harder to get up. My body was so
sore I couldn't touch a muscle. A few steps farther I went
down on my face in the middle of the road and this time
I couldn't get up.

I lay there for nearly two hours. I was afraid of falling
asleep for I knew that if I did I'd wake in the morning with
the sun in my eyes and a crowd of grinning Japs standing
over me. No matter how every nerve in my body rebelled,
I had to get up.

I tried but couldn't make it to my feet. I crawled on my
hands and knees off the roadside to a small tree. I managed
to pull myself to my feet by grasping the tree, but every
time I tried to take a step I fell down. I drew myself upright again and this time hung on to a branch and rocked
back and forth, trying to get the circulation going so that
my legs would support me. After some twenty minutes I
was able to let go of the tree and walk very slowly; my legs
felt as if they were dangling from my waist, I had so little
control of them.

When I dragged myself into the crevasse, I was too tired to sleep. I just sat in my chair and lay with my head on the table until daybreak.

Three days later, Antonio came up.

I smiled wanly. "I had a pretty good trip going down, but not so good coming back," I greeted him.

"What trip?" He wouldn't believe I'd gone all the way to Rojos' until he saw the blisters on my feet and the pictures, book, and maps I'd brought back.

It took me a week to get over my journey, but it was more than worth the trouble.

The quiz book gave me a great deal of pleasure. It contained nearly one hundred tests in all, one a day for over three months. In addition to general quizzes were bonus quizzes which gave extra points for correct answers, demerits for misses. I liked these complications. When you're living like Robinson Crusoe, the longer it takes to play a game the better.

There were special quizzes on labor, music, movies, radio, and other subjects. I was disappointed in the one on radio, because instead of testing my knowledge of transmitters, receivers, and frequencies, it asked such questions as "Who is Gracie Allen's husband?"

A feature I liked was the statement at the beginning of each test, telling how much a certain prominent person or expert in the field had scored on the same questions. It was a challenge, but, after all, how could I run up as high a score as Joan Crawford on questions about movie personalities?

I pored over the Rand McNally atlas for hours. There were colored drawings of North America, South America, Africa, Europe, and as a double spread in the middle of the book, a large map of the world. I spent a great deal of time on the pages showing the islands of the Pacific, but the one that I returned to day after day was the map of the United States.

I made a jigsaw puzzle of this map by placing onion skin over it and tracing the state borders. With the handsaw, I cut very thin pieces of wood, perhaps three-eighths of an inch thick, and with my pocketknife scraped them as smooth as ivory. I transferred the tracings to them and cut out the patterns of the various states. I whittled out all the forty-eight except Rhode Island. It was so small that I left it hanging on to Connecticut.

I spent many hours working and reworking the jigsaw. My chief interest wasn't in solving the puzzle, but in learning more about my country. After a while I could choose a state at random and without hesitation name all the states bordering it.

Another pastime I engaged in was tracing trails from one border of America to the other to see how many or how few states one could cross on a trip from the Pacific to the Atlantic Coast. The more familiar I became with these trails, the more they stirred my imagination. My mother lived near Beaverton, Oregon, a few miles outside Portland. Although Beaverton was not shown on the map, I estimated its location by using the scale, and put a dot there. Somehow it made my mother seem a little nearer. I had lived at Camas, Washington, one fall while working for a construction company. Camas was not on the map either, but I located and marked it.

I found the map a good peg on which to hang memories. I'd look a long time at the dot which stood for Grants Pass, in southern Oregon, where I lived as a boy. It was there that I used to roam the hills with my rifle, hunting rabbits, squirrels, and coyotes. It was partly because of these lonely expeditions that I was alive today. I followed the trail of my former travels up the Columbia River Highway and recalled the days spent in Astoria, Toledo, Tillamook and around Bend, Bountiful, and Hood River. The map with my dots on it seemed to bring all my daydreams nearer reality.

That map teased my imagination so that it had me making postwar tourist plans. I spent an entire week planning a coast-to-coast, Canada-to-Mexico tour of the United States. I told myself that when I got back I'd buy a house trailer, hitch it on behind my car, and see America first. I had done considerable traveling by water—been to Haiti, Costa Rica, and all through the Caribbean and the Pacific—but I wanted to travel on land, particularly my homeland. In my imaginary trailer I set out to visit every state in the Union. I'd tour northern states in the summertime and go south in the winter. I figured that when I got back home this would take some time. I wanted to spend at least a month in each of the forty-eight states. That would take four years. That was all right, I thought; I'd some day be retired from the Navy, and my retirement pay would be sufficient to take care of this extended trip. And as for time, what was time to me, perched out there on a rock in the middle of the Pacific?

PART THREE

THE RESCUE

19

IF I live to be 100 and anyone asks me what was the
most exciting moment of my life, I expect to answer
immediately, "June 11, 1944, the day the first American planes flew over Jap-held Guam."

The island had been alive with military activity during
the previous three months. In March the Japs had brought
over some 15,000 soldiers; in April they took about 5,000
away. In May they kept reinforcing the place until Guam
was bloated with probably more than 25,000 combat troops
as well as planes, artillery, tanks, and fuel. They were
building fortifications at strategic points all over the island.
Fifty-five Japs had come out to Juan Pangalinen's ranch
and constructed eleven emplacements for antiaircraft guns.
Three-quarters of a mile from my crevasse, they set up a
lookout station at a point overlooking the sea. All along
the coast from Machanao to Adelup Point, I could see shore
batteries firing practice shots.

By the second week in June they'd flown in hundreds of
aircraft. Planes by the dozens had whizzed overhead every
day since the middle of March. I was sick of seeing them.
When I heard one overhead, I didn't even bother to look up.

But June 11 was different. It was a cloudy, overcast day, and I was sitting inside at my table, but as soon as I heard the roar of these motors, I knew they were American bombers. They had a rhythm all their own, a deep, steady, reassuring pulse that by contrast made the whizzing Jap craft sound like cheap tin thrashing machines. I leaped to my feet and ran to the lookout.

I couldn't see them through the clouds, but that wonderful roar told me where they were. They circled the island and headed south. As I watched an opening in the clouds, bombers—big bombers—shot past, dropping slender, glittering silver fish.

Seeing the first big bomb splash in Agaña Harbor was like starting to live again! I knew that unless the Japs got me in a very short time, I'd be rescued. I got so excited I lost my footing on the narrow ledge and had to grab the limb of a tree behind me to keep from falling over the side of the 300-foot cliff.

I tried standing still and enjoying the scene and the sounds. It was the most beautiful music I had ever heard. Each time a bomb dropped, I'd say, "There's another for the lousy bastards!" They'd bombed us when we had no defenses. Now times had changed. They were getting a little of their own medicine. Things were going to be different around here—damned different!

Our fighter planes came over now and engaged the Japs in combat. American pilots swept in from the south, dropped bombs on Agaña Airfield, and shot northward over my lookout. Jap fighters came down from above, guns blazing. Machine-gun bullets chipped pieces off my cliff like hundreds of stonemasons working in spurts. I hid behind the rocks and peeped out. That night I really marked up my calendar. I put a big *W* in one square, *A* in the next, and *R* in the third.

In all the aerial combat, I never saw an American shot down. Jap planes plummeted to the earth like swatted flies. I'd follow the trail of a smoking Zero, watch it burst into flame and crash, and yell, "Hot damn! Another good Jap!"

When Antonio saw the bombings for the first time from the lookout, the Americans were hitting Cabras Island, Orote Peninsula, and Sumay.

"Gee!" he cried. "They're gonna blow up the whole island!"

As the American pilots flew over their targets, antiaircraft guns threw such a barrage of flak all around them that the sky looked as if it had been sprinkled with black pepper. These ground guns were more accurate than the Jap pilots. I saw them bring down five United States planes in one day. After the first two days, American pilots got wise to the location of the heaviest batteries and banked half a mile away from them before coming in for the kill.

Jap ground gunners kept pumping anyway at whatever they saw above them, whether it bore our white star or the red spot of the Rising Sun. Once, I distinctly saw two Jap planes take off from Agaña Airfield, fly out over the sea, climb to about 8,000 feet and circle back over the center of the island. The minute they were overhead, the Jap antiaircraft cut loose at them with everything they had.

Some five hundred Jap planes were there on Guam before the attack, ready to pounce on any invader. But it took only three days for our boys to clear the air of Japs; after that Americans dropped their bombs without the slightest opposition. About a week later the Japs brought in reinforcements. In two days United States planes had cleaned the sky again. From then on, there was virtually no resistance from the Jap air force.

On the fifth day of the battle I looked out to sea and saw several ships moving in from the north. I wasn't sure whether they were Americans or Japanese. Five ships cruised into view around the end of the island, six or eight miles out on the horizon. At first I thought they were battleships, but then I saw that they were large, improved heavy cruisers almost as big as the peacetime battleships I had known.

They kept coming. Destroyers and heavy cruisers sailed into view. I hoped they weren't Jap ships bringing support to the island garrison.

As soon as the gray force reached the coast opposite Agaña Bay, every ship opened fire. This was no Jap armada! "IT IS OUR NAVY!" I screamed. I was never so thrilled in my life! I wanted to plunge into the sea and swim out to them.

All Jap ships anchored outside the harbor were spotted by planes launched from the cruisers. Light seaplanes continually circled over the island all the time the cruisers were firing.

From then on, twin American destroyers passed my lookout every day as they circled the island. It wasn't until later that I learned they never were the same two.

Those ships gave me an even greater thrill than the airplanes. The planes had given me my first wild hope, but, after all, it was the good old Navy that would actually get me out.

But would they? I was afraid to let myself dwell on my

escape. If I didn't make it, the disappointment would kill me. But I'd try. By God, I'd try!

I ran down to my cabinet, took out a large oblong of gauze bandage Antonio had got from the dispensary, cut it in two, and nailed each half to a stick to make semaphore flags. Each one was about two feet square, large enough to be seen through binoculars if anyone, please God, on the ship happened to spot me.

As I scrambled back up to my lookout, I tried to recall the semaphore alphabet. I'd known it long before—it's regulation in the Navy. What had I been doing for the past two years? Why hadn't I spent them practicing signaling?

I couldn't figure it out now. The ships were moving. I frantically waved my flags up and down, up and down. Maybe somebody'd look my way.

I waved for fifteen minutes, rested, and waved again. No response. I'd hoped for too much on the first day. The ships were disappearing. They'd be back, though, maybe tomorrow. I had to get that alphabet. When I did catch their eye, I had to be able to tell them something!

I went back to my cave, stood there with a flag in each hand and concentrated. I got the first seven letters without any trouble. They were simple. But what message could I send with them? I figured out five more, twelve in all, that I could be sure of. I knew I'd have to do better than that. The majority of the letters had to be correct to make the message readable. I knew that if I were listening in over the radio and got a somewhat garbled code message I could still make it out if the key letters were right. The signalmen on those ships were experts. They'd fill in for me, if only I gave them enough to go on.

I worked for four days trying to remember that code. By

then, I felt pretty certain of nineteen letters, with seven still in doubt. There was a chance that my guesses on some of these seven were right. That was the best I could do. That—and pray for an expert receiver.

For a week, every time an American ship hove in sight I waved those flags. It was back-breaking work, emaciated as I was, but I kept it up for twenty minutes at a time, six or seven times a day. I knew that my only chance was that someone would scrutinize my area with his glasses. Most of the ships didn't stop, but cruised past at a steady pace from the north end of the island, to where I could no longer see them to the south. This took about twenty minutes, all of which I spent anxiously waving the gauze signals.

Trees in the distance cut off part of my view of the sea. I judged as carefully as I could just which ones they were, went down with my machete, and hacked away the tops. Now I had a clear swing of vision for 120 degrees. It gave a few seconds more in which I might be spotted from a ship. I brandished my white flags until my arms were sore, without results. What was the matter with those guys on the bridge?

Antonio came up, and I told him of my efforts. He was very worried. "You had better be careful," he said, "or those Japs over on the next hill might see you waving those white flags."

I knew that he was right. I had been unable to spot their lookout station so could not tell if they could see the cliff on which I was perched. If they ever saw me waving my white flags at the American warships it would not only be my finish but would also cost Antonio his life. He had endangered the lives of his family and himself for so long by

helping me that I could not, at this late date, bring almost
certain death to these people.

I had to quit signaling. I was bitterly disappointed.
Only a few miles stood between me and United States warships and I couldn't bridge that short distance.

But I'd be damned if I'd give up! I'd make a raft and
paddle out to them!

I figured out the number of bamboo pieces I'd need to
support me and the things I wanted to take. I doubted if
I'd have the strength to drag a raft all the way down to the
water's edge. I hadn't been as far away as the beach in
months. I didn't think I'd have the strength to make more
than a few trips loaded with bamboo, but I slipped down to
locate a place where I could build the raft in the water and
then keep it hidden there. There was no place to hide it. I
then decided to hide the bamboo in the bushes near the
water until the complete material was assembled and build
the raft in the water after dark. I could build it and leave
the island by two o'clock in the morning and be six or eight
miles offshore by daylight. Surely I would be picked up by
an American ship.

I went back home and started working on a paddle. I'd
make it kayak style, with a blade on each end. I could
make double time with that type, and every second counted
for me now.

When July 4 approached, I expected some special fire-
works. I wasn't disappointed. Beginning in early morning
our planes came over in raid after heavy raid. I shuttled
back and forth between my cave and lookout post every few
minutes to be sure I didn't miss anything.

On one trip I saw an American fighter plane flying a few
thousand feet over Agaña. I wished I were in it, headed

back for the carrier. At that moment, it was struck squarely amidships by antiaircraft fire; it smoked up, spluttered, and started down. It struck the water, exploded, and burst into flames. I was cursing the Japs for what they'd done when I saw a white blob mushroom in the sky above the plane and knew it was the pilot floating down in his parachute.

He landed in the bay four or five hundred yards off Agaña. The minute he struck, the Japs opened up with machine guns, shooting up white spurts of water all around him. Immediately ten American planes came in low over Agaña, bombing and strafing, making the Japs pull in their necks. I was afraid the pilot would be riddled, but then I thought, well, better to go down than have the lousy Japs get you.

The American planes kept up the strafing for half an hour, pulling the fire away from the pilot in the water. It seemed hopeless, though; they couldn't keep it up indefinitely; the Japs would get the pilot when the protecting planes went home. But finally a seaplane came in, dove on the town, strafed the machine gunners, circled back, and landed on the water alongside the pilot. The Jap guns really cut loose. The water was churned white by the bullets.

That little plane must have been perforated like a sieve, but apparently neither it nor its pilot was disabled. The flyer struggling in the water couldn't disentangle himself from his parachute. He wrapped his arms securely around the tail of the plane and it taxied through the water with him hanging on, his heavy parachute streaming out behind him in the water. Five hundred yards away, out from under the guns, they stopped and cut the parachute loose. There was not room for the man in the cockpit. The water-soaked pilot crawled out of the sea, lay down on the wing, and the plane took off. The rescue pilot flew only a few feet above the water, and very slowly, so that his buddy wouldn't roll off. They disappeared over the horizon. It was the best Fourth of July demonstration I'd ever seen.

The Americans developed a system of continual day and night attacks. Twenty or thirty ships, both cruisers and destroyers, would steam in about nine o'clock in the morning, shell the daylights out of a whole section of the beach, then sail out again after putting in a full eight-hour day. Two destroyers would stay on and bombard installations all night. They'd steam around the island, shelling as they went, just to keep the Japs awake and jumping.

The destroyers' firing technique was simple and effective. When they opened up, they'd fire the shells just as fast as they could load and let go. One night about one o'clock they opened up with a fierce bombardment right into our area. One shell dropped about a hundred feet from Antonio's house. It sprayed rocks and dirt into his cistern of drinking water. Several boulders struck the house where he and his frightened family shivered.

Next morning the Japs came to investigate and asked him if he'd drawn this fire by flashing lights out to sea. They warned him that he was under suspicion. When he was sure they weren't watching him, he came up to my cave and asked me to get rid of the semaphore flags entirely. He was afraid that the Japs watching his ranch might catch me trying to signal the American ships.

On July 10, the warships came in as usual, did their day's work, and pulled out. Late in the afternoon I saw that the two destroyers left behind for the night shift were about ten miles south of me. They were closer to shore than they'd ever been. They looked near enough for a man on board to hit the beach with a rock. My heart sank, for they stood almost under the muzzles of a battery of six- or eight-inch Jap guns mounted at Adelup Point.

I'd spotted the battery at target practice shortly before the Americans returned. I could tell that they were large guns from the flash they made, the distance the shells traveled before they splashed at sea, and the splash they made. I knew there were at least three guns in the emplacement, because I'd seen three flashes of fire so close together that they couldn't possibly have belonged to a second salvo. The Japs hadn't used these guns against the Americans so far, undoubtedly because they were saving them for our landing force and they didn't want to reveal their position. I held my breath because I knew they could outshoot the destroyers. A land-based gun is always more accurate than one mounted on a ship at sea. I prayed the Japs wouldn't open up on the destroyers now firing broadsides at the beach as they stood within point-blank range of the Jap battery. Finally they turned, unmolested, and started north in my direction.

I was worn out from the anxiety. It was getting on toward evening, and I had supper ready. I went back to the cave. I'd taken only a few bites when I heard the destroyers' guns firing very near, shooting almost straight in my direction. I'd learned that the sound of a gun firing in my direction is different from the report when it's pointed away. The projectile leaving the muzzle gives an extra, vicious "thug!" in addition to the regular report.

I grabbed my signal flags and pocket mirror. If they were close enough, I'd try a new plan. As I dashed up the cliff to the lookout, I heard an antiaircraft gun and a machine gun nest only two miles below me open fire on the destroyers. The ships' gunners quickly took the range of these Jap shore installations and blasted them to hell.

I had to admire the daring of the ships' commanders in coming so near the coast when they couldn't know what guns might be concealed there. They were hardly two miles from the shore, an easy, murderous range for large enemy guns. As they started right up past me, I scrambled to the very top of the cliff in plain view of the destroyers. With the little three-inch mirror I flashed a beam directly on the bridge of the leading ship. The late afternoon sun was in the sky right behind the warships so that I was sending them a powerful red flash. I danced the reflection all over the bridge. They must have seen it!

I threw down my mirror and grabbed up my signal flags. I waved the flags frantically up and down for possibly half a minute. Then I signaled, "Please answer by searchlight." I cannot read semaphore but am proficient in the reception of Morse code by lights. A signal searchlight winked from the bridge, "K," it said, code for "Go ahead!" I almost blew my top, but I forced myself to start out quite slowly and deliberately with my semaphore. I wanted them to get at least every letter I was sure of. They could figure out the rest. I'll always remember the exact words I sent.

"I have information for you."

Again this beautiful K winked across to me.

My head seemed to be going around in circles. I didn't know what I was doing or what I should do next. For a few minutes I manipulated my flags, but I have no idea what I said or whether the message was even intelligible.

I tried to warn them about the large battery that the Japs were holding back to use against our landing force. By now the bombardment of the island was so intense that I knew the landing would be made almost any day. I knew that if the battleships could blast that emplacement out of existence before the landing was attempted, it would save the lives of thousands of American troops.

When I finally calmed down and settled to a deliberate rate of sending, "The Japs have a battery of coast guns mounted at Adelup Point," I signaled.

Then I thought they ought to know that the Japs were killing pilots who made forced landings on the island. "The Japs kill every American who falls into their hands." I wanted the pilots to know what they were up against, so that they could either take a chance on crashing in the sea and being picked up by our ships or hit for the bush and hide out until the island fell if they were shot down inland.

The sun was still shining. The destroyers had slowed down when they spotted me on the cliff. They circled around one spot for probably half an hour while I talked to them. Finally, I'd given them all the information I knew— all I had about the strength and concentration of Jap troops on the island, the nature of off-shore barricades, mine fields, tank traps, and other obstructions, even some data on dummy guns. That was all. I was run down. The strain of trying to get the letters right was terrific.

I'd made no attempt whatever to identify myself. I knew they'd be suspicious. The first thing a spy would try to do would be to identify himself as a bona-fide American. If I told them nothing about myself but just gave them useful information, perhaps that would be in my favor.

I saw they were getting up speed. I was frantic. Through hot tears I slowly and distinctly spelled out, "Can you take me aboard?"

As I half-anticipated, I received no answer. That was all

I could expect, I thought, but I still stood there, too exhausted to stumble back to my cave.

Five minutes later, I saw a boat drop into the water.
That was answer enough for me! The people on that ship
knew I wasn't a Jap! How, I don't know. I didn't care.
I was practically delirious as I hoisted my flags for one final
message.

"Please wait for me. It will take me half an hour to get
down to the water."

I dropped the signal flags where I was, scooped up the
mirror, and stuck it in my pocket.

Inside my crevasse, I grabbed my machete, fastened on
my holster, opened the cracker can where I kept my pictures and records and stuffed them into my shirt front. I
slung the deer light Antonio had given me over my shoulder, and ran for the trail. I half-slid down the three rugged
cliffs, using both hands and feet to keep from falling. I
cracked my knees against the jagged corners of a shelf of
rock and took the hide off. I hardly felt it. I was down
by the water's edge in fifteen minutes. Never before had
I made it in less than three quarters of an hour.

I couldn't see the motor launch, but judged I was south
of it, since I had had to come slantwise down the cliff. I
didn't want them to think they were being drawn into a
trap. It was getting dark enough to signal with a light. I
tapped the end of the wire on the terminal of the battery so
that I could send code. First, I just flashed the light rapidly
several times.

The ship saw me and swung the signal light toward the
beach. "He is half a mile south of you," the signalman said.

Were they talking to me or to the boat? If to the boat,
I was turned around, and it was south of me.

"Are you talking to the boat or to me?" I flashed.

"To the boat."

Fine. Everything was as I'd figured it.

"Flash your light so the boat will spot you and know where to pick you up," they signaled to me.

I sent dots of yellow light north, and in a few minutes the launch came in sight.

"Here I am!" I shouted.

Meantime, I plumbed the water for depth. I found a place where it was a good eight feet, plenty deep enough to bring the boat right up to the shore. I didn't want to take any chances on that boat running aground.

I hurriedly snatched up my gear. Where was my pistol? I had forgotten it! I had been so crazy with excitement that I'd gone off and left the one object that had never left my side, day or night, in two whole years. It was too late now. I couldn't go back for it. The boat was within two hundred yards of me.

But it didn't come in. I could see it dimly.

"Come on in! There's plenty of water here!" I shouted to them.

"No, you swim out."

"I can't. I've got too much gear."

"Leave the gear."

There was plenty of water for the boat to come in right to the rock on which I was standing. I didn't want to get my pictures and records wet by swimming.

"You have eight feet of water right here where I'm standing!"

"We are *not* coming in. Swim out and leave your gear there."

"I can't leave it here. The Japs'll find it and kill the man who owns this place." I felt that the Japs must have seen the two destroyers circling in this spot for so long. It was endangering Antonio's life. I could not leave anything behind for that would make his death certain.

"We are not coming in!"

I was worried. I didn't answer. These people were going to get disgusted and return to the ship. Then the Japs, seeing the two destroyers circling this spot, would come out here to look for me. I must get away!

"You swim out. If *you're* all right, then we'll come in and get your things," someone finally shouted.

"Oh, it's *me* you're afraid of!"

"You ain't just a-lying!" I heard one of the fellows in the boat say.

I dropped everything and started tearing off my clothes. Although it was getting dark fast, there was still some light, and when I'd stripped to the hide I heard someone in the boat say, "He *looks* like a white man."

We'd been there so long, making so much noise arguing about the gear, and with the warships circling in that same spot offshore, that I was afraid a Jap patrol might be on its way down there.

"Has anybody there got a gun?" I called out.

No answer.

"I say, has anybody got a gun!" I cried out louder.

No answer. They weren't giving away any information.

"Well, if you have, and you see anybody besides me, let 'em have it. They'll be Japs!"

I swam out to the boat.

When they saw I was really white, two dozen arms reached out for me. They pulled me over the side, and I fell sprawling into the boat. Once aboard, I saw that the thirty men bristled with enough submachine guns to wipe out an entire Jap platoon.

I'll never forget how good it felt to get back with Americans, hear Americans, see Americans, especially Navy men like myself. They were the best looking bunch of men I ever saw in my life. Every one of them had a question.

"Where've you been?"

"Where'd you come from?"

"How long've you been there?"

When I told them I'd been hiding from the Japs on the island for over two years and a half, they didn't believe me. They thought I was a pilot who'd been forced down a week or two previously. One look at me should have convinced them I was telling the truth. I looked like a wild animal. I was naked. My shaggy hair hung almost down to my shoulders. I hadn't shaved for three days.

We went back to shore for my things. On the way the men peeled their own clothes off their backs and threw them over to me. I took a shirt. I put on my own trousers, homemade shoes, and underwear.

I'd never received such a welcome as I got from these Navy men. When we pulled up alongside the ship, they lowered the blocks from the davits, hooked the boat on, and hoisted her up with everybody in it. When we were level with the destroyer's deck, the men in the boat pushed me forward to be the first man out. "Jump on over!" somebody yelled. Half a dozen fellows gave me a helping shove from behind, and half a dozen more caught me as I hit the deck.

One of the six was Commanding Officer, Lt. Comdr. J. B. Carroll. He shook hands, congratulated me, and thanked me for the information I'd sent.

"You got here in the nick of time. We're just sitting down to eat," he said, inviting me to officers' mess.

I sat beside Commander Carroll. There were electric lights, white table linen, china, and silver in an immaculate cabin within a few miles of my hole in the cliff. There was a baked ham, green vegetables, and bread and butter. I hadn't seen bread and butter more than half a dozen times while I was in the bush. Many times in my cave when I was cooking supper I had thought I'd gladly swap everything I had to eat, including all my canned goods, for just one good thick slice of white bread spread with a deep layer of yellow butter.

I was too excited to eat much. I stuffed down some bread and a small helping of green vegetables. That was all.

I made a diagram for Commander Carroll, showing him the exact location of the battery of coast guns.

"You don't know how lucky you are," he said. "After we had blasted that Jap antiaircraft and machine gun out of existence we came on up the coast, where we spotted the reflection of your mirror. The way you quivered it, it looked exactly like gun flashes. When I saw them I said, 'Aha! Another Jap gun getting smart with us.' We took your range and bearing, trained our guns on you, and were ready to open fire when, at the last second, you dropped the mirror and began waving your flags. Somebody shouted, 'Hold everything! I think someone is trying to signal to us.' If you'd waited another second to start waving your flags, you'd have been blown to hell."

Lieutenant Butler, the medical officer, took me to his office for a once-over. He found nothing wrong; said I'd survived my ordeal pretty well.

"Now," he said significantly. "Is there anything you'd like especially?"

"A shower!" I said fervently.

"Okay. But don't you have a little cough?" he asked in a voice full of meaning. "We're well equipped," he added.

I caught on. I coughed. "Doctor, I've had considerable difficulty with my throat lately," I complained.

"Swell! I've the very thing to fix you up!"

He reached into a cabinet and came out with a pint of bonded rye whiskey.

"Drink this. It'll do you good."

I took one swallow and returned the bottle.

"Go ahead, help yourself," he urged, but I'd not had a drink in so long that I knew it wouldn't take much to set me spinning.

He then led the way into the officers' washroom, and left to get me some clean clothes.

I left my old ones in a filthy heap on the floor and stepped into the luxury of a powerful stream of hot water beating down on my body.

When Lieutenant Butler came back, I was still under the shower. I didn't ever want to get out.

"Take your time," he called in.

As a matter of fact, the actual scrubbing necessary to scrape off the layers and layers of dirt which I imagined were caked on my body in the course of two and a half years in the dusty bush and crude cave, took plenty of time. That soap and shower brush took a heluva beating. I stepped out feeling brand new.

"What's that awful stench?" I asked. Then I saw my dirty clothes piled on the floor at my feet. "My God, if

I'd fished up from the ocean anything smelling like that, I'd have thrown it back!"

I put on the clean underwear Lieutenant Butler handed me, grabbed up that pile of dirty clothes and made for the deck to throw them overboard. A dozen men almost knocked me down to keep me from doing it. I was as surprised as hell to see them fight over those smelly clothes for souvenirs. One shoe went one way, its mate, the other.

We went back to Lieutenant Butler's quarters. He gave me the first socks I'd had in over a year, and a fine pair of black shoes that one of the men had sent up as a present to me, without even leaving his name.

The doctor laid out two clean uniforms, one khaki and one gray. I'd never seen the gray before. It'd been adopted by the Navy after Guam was taken by the Japs.

"Who wears that one? I like it," I said, pointing to the gray.

"It's for officers and chiefs."

"Oh, in that case, I'll have to take the khaki. I'm not a chief yet—still first class."

"Well, the khaki's for officers and chiefs, too, so you might as well wear the gray," he laughed.

Once dressed, I looked at myself in the narrow mirror in the door and thought that if I could just get rid of that three days' growth of beard and my almost three years' growth of hair down my back, perhaps I could begin to look human again.

"All men who were in the landing party report immediately!" the call came out over the loud-speaker.

The group gathered in the wardroom, and the ship's photographer took pictures.

For the rest of the evening we sat around talking. The fellows gave me cigarettes, matches, chewing gum, in every way showing me that they were glad I'd lived to tell my story and was there with them now. Now it was my time to ask questions.

"Is Germany knocked out yet? Where is General McArthur now? Why has it taken so long for the Americans to get back to Guam?"

They brought me up to date, telling me about the major war fronts that had developed since early 1942 when I had to abandon my radio, shutting myself off from the outside world. They explained the priorities that the European war front had on men and materials, causing the long delay in the rescue of our far-flung Pacific outpost. They told me proudly about the big task force, of which they were a part, that was now sweeping across the Pacific, giving the Japs hell wherever they had established garrisons. All the men were full of confidence.

When it was time to turn in, Lieutenant Butler showed me to a bunk in the officers' quarters. I undressed and eased into the finest bed I'd felt since the Beauty Rest mattress at Tommy Tanaka's in September, 1942.

I heaved a big sigh of relief, closed my eyes, and for the life of me couldn't fall asleep. There were no mosquitoes, no ants, no leaks in the roof, no rain in my face. No wonder I couldn't drop off! Actually, I was just too excited to quiet down and give up.

I put on my clothes and went to the radio room. The chief let me take over for a while and handle some messages. It felt good to know I hadn't lost my know-how at the key. I fanned the breeze with the operators on watch and paced

The view from my lookout.

My first American bread in over two years.

I had $6,000 in back pay.

The Admiral made me a Chief.

the deck, breathing sea air again and thanking God for my escape.

Next morning before breakfast I was transferred to an aircraft carrier where an admiral, captains, and Naval Intelligence questioned me all day. My throat became so sore and inflamed that I could only whisper. I'd talked so little during the past year and nine months that my vocal cords just couldn't take it.

Admiral Clark, in command of the naval aircraft bombing Guam, detailed a chief yeoman to look after me. When he kept making appointments for me one right after another, I objected. A man has some rights. "I can't go see these big shots with hair on my shoulders and my beard bristling," I said.

He ignored me. His mind was on satisfying the gold braid. Finally, between conferences, I ducked into the chiefs' quarters.

"Anybody here lend me a razor?"

About a dozen men leaped up and offered me all kinds of shaving equipment. I went to the washroom and shaved, accompanied by the protesting chief.

"Now, I'm going to get a haircut," I informed the chief. He was biting his nails and shifting from one foot to another.

"The Executive Officer wants to see you," he insisted.

"I've looked like a tramp long enough. Where's the barber shop?" was my reply.

"Okay, okay, I'll fix that immediately," he promised. "Come on."

We went by the shop, picked up the barber, and took him along with us. In the Executive Officer's quarters, I

sat on a stool, the barber cut my hair, the Executive Officer
and I carried on our business to the satisfaction of all concerned. It looked to me as if the Navy had changed a lot.

As the chief and I left, he said, "Admiral Clark told me
to see that you get a complete outfit of clothing."

"I don't want to buy many clothes now," I told him. "I
took an examination for chief radioman in October, 1941,
before the war started, and I don't want to get a complete
outfit of clothes as radioman first class and then have to
throw them away and buy new chief's uniforms. I want
to wait until I find out if I made chief."

He left, saying he would find out about it. After a few
minutes he returned and said, "The admiral wants to see
you."

When we entered the Admiral's cabin, he shook hands
with me and said, "Hello, chief, how are you making out?"

"I beg your pardon, Admiral, but I am still radioman
first class."

"You *were* radioman first class, Tweed, but now you are
chief radioman. I heard about that examination you took
and whether you made it or not I'm making you chief from
this minute on."

"Thank you, Admiral," I managed to say. I was choked
up inside. This was the United States Navy I had come
back to—the greatest Navy in the world—and the people in
it the swellest anywhere.

After being completely outfitted with chief's summer uniforms and a complete outfit of toilet articles, I was informed by the chief that the entire outfit was "on the admiral." He had instructed the chief to see that I was completely outfitted at his expense.

A few minutes later I was taken to the pay office. The Disbursing Officer said, "Tweed, I hear you have some back pay coming. I don't think I will go into the higher reaches of mathematics to figure out how much. You had better wait until you get back to the States for that, but here is $250 clothing allowance for making chief."

At the close of our conversation, the Commander asked, "Do you like to fly?"

I thought they might be considering transferring me to Naval Aviation.

"I don't mind how high I fly, sir, so long as I can keep one foot on the deck," I replied.

He laughed. "We're transferring you to a flagship at Saipan," he told me. "You're going right away; so get ready and get out on deck."

I was catapulted off the deck in a TBF bomber and landed an hour later at Saipan. Then a motor launch took me to another ship, Vice-admiral Turner's flagship, anchored offshore.

Word had reached the Admiral that I had served under him aboard the *U.S.S. Saratoga* when he was its executive officer. When I entered his cabin, he turned to a commander and two lieutenants standing by and ordered, "Get the hell out of here. I want to talk to an old shipmate!"

"Who the hell rated you chief?" thundered the Admiral, after we had talked for a moment.

My heart sank. Was he displeased that I had been rated chief? I began to wonder if I had made it on the examination.

"Admiral Clark did, sir," I answered.

"Well, that old so-and-so. I wanted to do that myself."

After I had talked with Admiral Turner for half an hour, he said, "Tweed, I am going to send you back to the States as fast as our planes can get you there. You have been away a long time and I know you will be glad to get back home."

It's a grand Navy!

PART FOUR

THE RETURN

20

IT IS the disappointment of my life that I missed the re-
taking of Guam. All of us on the island had lived for
that day. Night after night in the cave at Manuel Cruz's
place, discussions had ended, "Wait 'til the Americans
come back. Just wait!" That thought kept hope alive in
an island of people. I'd done plenty of thinking about the
sweet revenge I'd take when I finally got a machine gun in
my hands.

But the Navy had other plans for me. While the Marines were landing on Guam, I was sitting in front of a
radio, in San Diego, California, listening for the news of the
invasion. My only consolation was that they landed with
all the information I could give. The Americans landed on
the island eleven days after I escaped. All the time I was
flying from Guam to Pearl Harbor to San Francisco to
Washington, with interviews by Intelligence officers at every
stop, and while I went from war plant to war plant giving
"incentive talks," I kept worrying about my friends I had
left behind, especially Antonio. I wrote an official letter to
the Island Commander of Guam, sending it through the
Chief of Naval Operations, requesting information as to the

welfare of Antonio, Josefa, and the children. The letter
went air mail and in a special pouch, and so when I received
no answer, I was afraid the Japs had closed in on the Arteros before the Americans landed.

Then the Navy suggested that I return to Guam, do a
short tour of duty for them, and find out for myself about
my friends. That suited me fine.

I left Washington by plane on Monday, September 18,
stayed two days at Pearl Harbor, long enough to pick up a
letter from Admiral Nimitz requesting I be given all the
assistance possible in completing my mission on Guam. We
sighted the island on the afternoon of Sunday the 24th. I'd
never flown over it and was eager to see Agaña from the
air, but we stayed seaward until we passed the town. As
we came in to Sumay Peninsula, I looked for the Marine
Barracks and the town of Sumay, but couldn't spot either.
We landed on an entirely new airport; it was like coming
in to a strange place.

"Where's the Marine Barracks?" I asked a mechanic on
the field.

"You mean 'Where *was* it,'" he said. He pointed toward
one end of the airfield. "It used to be there. Jap machine
gunners used it for cover; we had to crack down on it."

I telephoned headquarters in Agaña, and they sent a jeep
out for me. It was eleven miles in to town, and we were
halfway there before I found a landmark that I recognized,
the island was so torn up. Roads had been changed and
widened, and what used to be towns before the war were
now Army and Marine encampments or just rubble.

Agaña was a ghost town. What had been a neatly
planned city lay before me a jumble of wreckage, with

chunks of concrete buildings strewn everywhere. Occasionally I'd spot a piece of tin that used to be on a roof.

I went directly to the Island Command located in a tent city on the hill above Agaña. I was assigned to the transient officers' tent. Quarters were crude. If you wanted to wash your face, you borrowed a helmet, filled it with water, and used it for a basin. I didn't mind that. I'd had worse accommodations on Guam. It had been raining, and the inside of the tent was damp and the dirt floor was muddy. One of the men pointed to a pool of water just outside the door and said, "Every time it rains, that mud puddle backs up to the tent so we can swing out and wash our feet in it!"

I proceeded with caution to find Antonio, because I was informed that a large number of Jap soldiers were still at large, most of them hiding in the bush in the northern section. I didn't want to broadcast that Antonio'd sheltered me as long as there was any chance of danger to him. Afraid to make direct inquiries, I thought of Mrs. Johnston. She could tell me whether it was generally known how much Antonio had helped me.

I found Mrs. Johnston at the American Red Cross Headquarters kneeling beside a pile of clothes which she was sorting. I went over to her; she looked up at me without a sign of recognition in her face. I wasn't surprised. It had been two years, while I was still at Manuel Cruz's cave, since she had seen me. I was thinner now and cleanshaven, had a fresh haircut, and had exchanged my old blue shirt and ragged blue dungarees for a new khaki warrant officer's uniform.

I said, "I am looking for Mrs. Johnston."

"That's me," she answered, but still she didn't even recognize the sound of my voice.

Several native girls in other parts of the room were curious and left their work to stand behind us, listening. I smiled at Mrs. Johnston for a minute and asked her, "Did you ever know a man named Tweed?" She took a good look then, and all of a sudden jumped up and grabbed my hand and held it and cried out so everyone could hear, "This is Tweed! It's Tweed!" One of the girls fainted.

All the Chamorros gathered round, everybody reaching out at the same time to shake my hand, telling me how glad they were to see me back again. They'd read of my escape in *Life*.

I took Mrs. Johnston aside and asked her about Antonio. She said that everybody knew he'd been responsible for me and there was no further need for secrecy. Antonio, Josefa, and all the family were safe, she told me, living for the present on a cousin's ranch at Tutujan, only a mile from Agaña, while the Americans cleared the Japs out of the area around his own ranch. Mrs. Johnston knew the way, and so we climbed into the jeep supplied me by the Island Command and drove out to the house. We stopped in the ranch yard, and as I stepped out Antonio saw me, came running out, threw his arms around me, and started crying. Josefa followed him and wept, too. We embraced, saying nothing. This was the day we'd all looked forward to for so long.

I met their children for the first time. They'd never been told that I was staying on their father's ranch. Antonio explained that the Japs closed in on his ranch two days after I'd escaped. From him and from later talks with Juan Flores I got the whole story. Flores had learned from his brother, Joaquín, that I had gone to Pangalinen's place. Months later, when the Japs were putting on terrific pressure to hunt me down, he was afraid he might be caught and killed for what he knew. He was a good Catholic and was afraid it might be a mortal sin to possess the knowledge of my movements and keep it secret. He felt that he was facing death and went to the confessional and told Father Duenas that I had gone to Pangalinen's ranch. "Father," he asked, "is it a sin to keep this secret?"

"No, my son. Do not tell anybody."

But Father Duenas himself left the confessional booth and told so many people that he knew where I had gone that word got to the Japs. They tortured him until he finally broke down and told them I had gone to Pangalinen's.

The Japs were furious that Father Duenas had not reported his knowledge earlier. They killed the priest.

On the day after the Navy boat picked me up and took me away from the island, the Japs went to Pangalinen's and tortured him until he told them that he thought I'd gone to Antonio's.

After they dragged it out of him that he'd seen me recently for a few minutes and had not reported it, they tied him to a tree. When Juan, a strong man, saw they meant to kill him, he broke his bonds and started running across an open field to the bushes. The Japs fired and missed. He fell on his face to dodge their bullets and they ran and caught him. They tied him up again and cut off his head.

Next morning, the Japs ordered Juan Flores and Limtiaco to bring Antonio and his family into headquarters. With the example of Juan Pangalinen fresh in their minds, they were scared to within an inch of their lives. They went to

Antonio's house and told him that the Japs were putting everybody in concentration camps so that no help could be given the Americans who were now bombing and strafing the island. "You and all your family must report to Jap headquarters at once." Antonio could see from their nervousness that they weren't telling him the whole story. "We've stuck together all this time; it's only a matter of days before the Americans will drive the Japs out. Let's keep on helping each other until the end. What is it you're holding back?"

Even though failing might mean their deaths, they couldn't go through with it. They admitted to Antonio that the Japs were certain that he'd been feeding me all this time and wanted him and his family in order to kill them. Antonio said, "The only thing I can do is hide my family in the bushes. We must have food. It'll take me a while to get it out there. Take your time going back. Tell the Japs you couldn't find me, that there's nobody home here. Give me a chance."

Antonio and his brother José hurriedly got together some rice and other food, took Josefa and the eight children, and set out for my hiding place in the cliffs. Juan and Limty went slowly back to Agaña, so that when the Japs threw a ring around the ranch and closed in, the family was gone.

The crevasse that had been large enough for one was cramped quarters for eleven. The only dry place to sleep was under the shelter I'd built for my bed. Josefa and the younger children slept there. The others piled *fiderico* leaves on the ground and lay on them. They were soaked by rain almost every night. They had hard going. The youngest child, only ten months old, cried a great deal. José got jittery. He was afraid the baby's crying would lead the Japs to them. After three weeks, José went temporarily mad. He grabbed Josefa, slammed her up against the rock cliff, waved his machete and threatened to cut off all their heads. Antonio heard the ruckus from outside, rushed in and calmed his brother.

On the twenty-fourth day, they ran out of food, and Antonio set out to forage. He was afraid the Japs would kill him, but he couldn't let his family starve. As he was sneaking up to his house, he was surprised from behind by a patrol—not Japs, but Americans. They brought the family down safely to Tutujan, where they were now living until all the Japs could be driven out of their ranch.

When he finished, Antonio and Josefa insisted that I stay with them. It took no urging to get me to transfer my headquarters out of the muddy tent at the Island Command, to the house of my friends.

I was eager to revisit my hideout, and went to the Island Command for permission. It was refused, because such a trip was too dangerous; the Japs were scattered all through the area. They didn't hold any part of it, but individual snipers made daylight raiding so expensive that the Americans did all their Jap killing at night. Their chief method was to post ambushes on roads and trails, with orders to shoot everything that moved. Natives understood this and stayed in. About thirty-five Japs were killed every night.

I insisted to Island Command that one of my assignments was to take pictures of the hideout. They finally agreed, but put their foot down when it came to letting me go alone, detailing a patrol to accompany me.

Antonio, José, and a Navy photographer went with us. I led the way, still hoping to flush a few Japs. We passed within about fifty yards of a deserted ranch house where

I thought some might be hiding. One of the soldiers said, "There's none in there." I asked him how he knew. "Because we're on the leeward side, and if there were any we could smell them." I thought he was kidding, but one of the other men said, "That's right; if Japs were in there, your nose would tell you."

When we reached the bottom of the cliff below the hideout, we went more carefully. Some Japs might have found the place and be living in it. I went ahead, climbing as cautiously as possible, and sneaked to the shelter entrance, as I had often pictured a Jap detail slipping up on me before I had rigged up my alarm system. I stepped up on the last ledge, my rifle ready, and peered in. It was just as it had been before I left—table, chair, stool, everything—and not a Jap in sight. In all this time they still hadn't found it.

I signaled below, and the party came up. We were all panting and sweating from the climb. I stripped off my shirt and wrung about a quart of water out of it. We took several pictures. They were all posed, of course, but they were true to life. We took shots of me sitting at the table studying, on the mat making shoes, and standing at the lookout. My undershirt and trousers were cleaner now. I wore Army shoes, and I had a shave and haircut, but otherwise they might have been made six months before.

On the way back, we found a dead Jap. Antonio said that he and José and two others had come along this trail some days previously. When they had drawn near the well, they had seen this Jap approaching it from the other side. Antonio took a bead on him but was reluctant to kill a man, even a Jap, and didn't fire. José saw Antonio pointing his gun, and then saw the Jap. José took aim and let fly. The report made Antonio jump, and he pulled the trigger. Both bullets went through the Jap's chest. He was still lying in the same spot where he had fallen.

Naturally, Tommy Tanaka was high on my list of people to look up, but I had trouble locating him. One morning before breakfast he showed up at Antonio's. He didn't look well, as he was recovering from an attack of dinghy fever.

One of the first things Tommy said was, "Mrs. Dejima knew all the time that I was carrying food out of her store to you. She told me to help myself to anything in the place."

"Let's go see her right now," I said.

We drove in the jeep to the stockade where all full-blooded Japanese were being kept for investigation, and they brought out Mrs. Dejima. She looked well and seemed in good spirits. I thanked her for everything she'd done for me and promised to do whatever I could to obtain her release. We asked if there was anything else she wanted. Yes, she said, there was. She'd buried some valuables out near Yigo and she'd like to have them but was afraid the Americans might take them away from her. What did I think?

I told her she had absolutely nothing to fear, that Americans didn't operate the way Japs did. If she wanted to get her things, she'd be allowed to keep them. She was very pleased, and I arranged to take her out the following day.

Next morning, Tommy and I went in the jeep to the stockade, where I signed up for Mrs. Dejima, and we headed for Yigo. We got a patrol of about fifteen men there, for the area was lousy with Japs, making it one of the most dangerous parts of the island. When they'd first taken to the bushes, they'd forced about two hundred natives to carry food and ammunition for them. When they were far enough away in the hills to keep the natives from rushing their hiding place, they lined them up and, one by one, decapitated the whole two hundred.

Mrs. Dejima directed us through the woods to a spot under a tree. It was like looking for buried treasure. I dug out seven wrist-watches and a bracelet of rubies and diamonds. The only precaution she'd taken was to wrap them in cellophane, which had rotted. Dirt was caked around the jewels and winding stems, and the watches were probably beyond repair.

Half a mile farther on, she pointed out another spot, and, about two feet from the surface, I uncovered a coffee can. We peeled off the paint with which the lid was sealed on, and opening the can we saw that it contained a smaller can also sealed with paint. It was full of American money, as fresh and clean as when she'd put it there. She'd buried over ten thousand dollars in good old American money.

The island was so torn up, families so scattered, and time so short that I was being hard put to it to see all my friends. We found Manuel Aguon at his ranch, near a large camp set up at Manengon. I wanted especially to see him to ask about Krump. If anybody knew whether the chief had been caught, he would. Manuel said, "Yes, Krump was with the other two, and all three were executed."

Manuel brought out some *tuba* for us to drink, and we had a long visit. When I left, he gave me half a bag of bananas.

I was determined to keep my date with Juan Mendiola.

Friends had told me he'd kept his promise not to take a drink until the Japs were run out. I found him in charge of men working in the galley at one of the Marine camps. I brought out a quart of Johnny Walker which I had carried with me all the way from Pearl Harbor for the occasion, and Juan invited a couple of his friends over to his house for a party. We didn't get drunk, but we had enough to celebrate on.

Before leaving, I saw everybody who'd helped me—Juan Cruz, Sus Mesa, Joaquín Flores, and all the others. I even got the recipe for Sus Quitugua's wonderful pancakes that were one of my few bright spots during my thirty-one months in the bush.

Of all the ones I looked forward to seeing, I was fondest of Tonie, the girl who had come to see me at Yoña and at Tumon. One of her best friends told me a story that almost broke my heart. When Tonie had brought me food, she'd been seen by Sus Reyes. Soon afterward the Japs caught him and tortured him. About the same time they dragged in Tonie and charged her with helping me. She denied everything until they brought in Reyes, who confronted her with accusations she couldn't deny. They whipped her with telephone wire until her back and legs were crisscrossed with bleeding stripes. Then they wrapped her head in a towel and flooded her face with water, leaving her half-drowned and unconscious. She came to with water running out of her nose and mouth and ears. She looked down at her leg. A Jap had kicked her with his hobnailed boots and split the flesh open so the bone showed. She was nearly dead when they let her mother come for her.

They left Tonie alone until the American warships started

bombarding the island.   Many Chamorros fled to the hills
to escape shellfire.   Tonie, her friend Beatrice Perez, and
several others ducked into a cave where Jap soldiers had
taken shelter.   The Japs held them there for a day and a
half, charged them with being American spies, and con-
demned them to death.   They took them out and lined them
up in front of two shallow shell holes; the seven men by
one, the four women by the other.

One girl made a break and ran.   A dozen Japs dashed
after her and brought her back.   A Jap officer gave an order
and they stripped her to the waist.   He shouted again and a
soldier raised his sword and cut away one of her breasts as
she stood screaming.   She was left standing there to die.

Tonie was next.   A Jap slit open her stomach with his
bayonet and pulled out her intestines.   She remained standing for two or three minutes, then toppled over.

Beatrice saw a Jap soldier run toward her, bayonet raised.
As she closed her eyes, the Jap slammed the bayonet down
across the back of her neck and she fell into the shell hole.

Some time later Beatrice came to.   She was covered with
earth, only her hand sticking out.   After an eternity of struggling, she drew herself to her knees, pushed away the dirt,
and got to her feet.   She heard a faint cry.   It was Tonie.
She, too, had struggled from her grave and was calling for
help.   Beatrice managed to drag her to the top of the shell
hole, when Tonie collapsed and died in her arms.

After a stay of three weeks, I left on October 15.   As my
plane flew north, I took my last look at Guam.   It seemed
the same as when I first saw it from the Navy transport in
August, 1939.   The foliage crowding the white beach and
the high cliffs of Machanao hadn't changed.   But they

meant a lot more to me. I knew that island now. I knew that land from having crawled over it on hands and knees. I understood the Chamorros, having seen them suffer. And I knew that these people were as brave and loyal as any who ever lived under the American flag.